This book is due for return on or before the last date shown below.

10/02/06		
15/05/08		
3 oct 08		
7 Jan 09		
01 June 09		
9 5 - 1 10		
15 Nov 10		
1/5/13		

Richmond Adult Community College Library

C

0208 843 7928

D1757267

RACC LIBRARY

16289

148

Sybold van Ravesteyn
Tischlampe / table lamp
1926
32,7 x 15,5 x 17 cm
vernickeltes Metall; lackiertes Holz; Bakelit; Porzellan /
nickel-plated metal; lacquered wood; bakelite; porcelain
Collection Vitra Design Museum, Weil am Rhein

Nach seinem Studium in Delft machte Sybold van Ravesteyn Bekanntschaft mit Gerrit Rietveld vom De Stijl und
mit El Lissitzky, dem Mitbegründer des Konstruktivismus
in Russland – außerdem besuchte er das Bauhaus in
Dessau. In diesem Entwurf von fast brutaler Einfachheit
haben die Begegnungen mit den funktionalistischen
Avantgarden der Zeit deutliche Spuren hinterlassen.

After his studies in Delft, Sybold van Ravesteyn became
acquainted with Gerrit Rietveld of De Stijl and with
El Lissitzky, the co-founder of Russian Constructivism,
and also visited the Bauhaus in Dessau. This design,
characterized by an almost brutal simplicity, clearly bears
the mark of his encounters with these members of the
era's functionalist avant-garde.

149

Armstuhl / armchair
No. 9 (6009)
ca. 1899/1900
Gebr. Thonet, Wien
77 x 59 x 54,5 cm
gebogenes Buchenholz, gefärbt; Rohrgeflecht / bent
beechwood, stained; canework
Collection Alexander von Vegesack, Lessac-Confolens

Mitte der 1920er Jahre wurde Thonets einfacher Caféhaus-
stuhl von der Avantgarde als ökonomisches Wohnmöbel
neu entdeckt. Die universelle Funktionalität dieses In-
dustrieprodukts, das sich in jahrzehntelangem, massen-
haftem Gebrauch bewährt hatte, wurde besonders
medienwirksam von Le Corbusier herausgestellt, als er
den Stuhl 1925 zusammen mit seinen *Casiers Standards*
zur Möblierung des *Pavillon de l'Esprit Nouveau* nutzte.

In the mid-1920s, Thonet's simple coffee house chair
was rediscovered by the avant-garde as an economical
furniture piece for the home. Having proven its value
through decades of mass-scale usage, the universal
functionality of this industrial product was highlighted
by Le Corbusier to considerable media acclaim when he
used the chair in combination with his *Casiers Standards*
to furnish the 1925 *Pavillon de l'Esprit Nouveau*.

150

Le Corbusier, Pierre Jeanneret, Charlotte Perriand
Armsessel / armchair
Fauteuil à dossier basculant (Vorserie / preliminary series)
1928
Le Corbusier, Pierre Jeanneret, Charlotte Perriand, Paris
64 x 64 x 66,6 cm
verchromtes Stahlrohr; Leder; Stahlfedern /
chromium-plated tubular steel; leather; steel springs
Collection Vitra Design Museum, Weil am Rhein

Wie Adolf Loos lehnte auch Le Corbusier eine künstlerisch
beeinflusste Gestaltung ab und propagierte Gegenstände,
deren Formen sich aus einem evolutionären Prozess von
Produktion und Gebrauch ergeben. So traten die wenigen
Möbel, deren Entwurf er selbst mit verantwortete, als
zeitgenössische Fassungen bekannter Möbeltypen auf.
Quelle dieses Fauteuils mit beweglicher Rückenlehne ist
die Grundform eines zerlegbaren Reisesessels.

Like Adolf Loos, Le Corbusier rejected artistically
influenced design and propagated objects whose forms
resulted from an evolutionary process of production and
use. Hence, the few furniture designs that he himself
helped shape were contemporary versions of well-known
furniture types. The design for this wingback chair with
a flexible backrest was taken from the basic form of a
knockdown travel chair.

151

Walter Gropius, Adolf Meyer
Türklinke / door-handle
1922
S.A. Loevy, Berlin
6 x 14 x 11,5 cm
Nickellegierung, gegossen / nickel alloy, casted
Collection Alexander von Vegesack, Lessac-Confolens

Aus zusammengesetzten geometrischen Grundformen
entwickelt, zeigt dieser gemeinsame Entwurf von Walter
Gropius, dem Gründungsdirektor des Bauhaus, und
Adolf Meyer bereits Einflüsse der holländischen De Stijl-
Künstler um Theo van Doesburg und Piet Mondrian.

Developed from a combination of basic geometric forms,
this joint design by Walter Gropius, the founding director
of the Bauhaus, and Adolf Meyer shows the emerging
influence of the Dutch De Stijl artists surrounding Theo
van Doesburg and Piet Mondrian.

152

Max Bill & Hans Gugelot
Hocker / stool
1954
Hochschule für Gestaltung Ulm, Ulm
44 x 39,1 x 29,6 cm
Fichte; Buche / spruce; beech
Collection Vitra Design Museum, Weil am Rhein

Im kollektiven Gedächtnis steht dieses spartanische
Möbel stellvertretend für die Hochschule für Gestaltung
Ulm, an der zusammen mit ehemaligen Bauhäuslern eine
Designausbildung entwickelt wurde, die Kunst und Technik auf wissenschaftliche Forschung gründete. Als ein
typisches Produkt der Schule erschließt dieses Objekt
gerade durch die formale Minimierung sofort seine
Funktion: in diesem Fall als Beistelltisch oder als Hocker
sowie – mit der Stange als Tragegriff – als Tablett.

In the collective memory, this Spartan piece of furniture
is emblematic of the Ulm School of Design, where a design
education curriculum embracing scientific research
as the foundation of art and technology was developed in
conjunction with former Bauhaus members. A typical
product of the school, this object embodies a minimization
of form that immediately demonstrates its function—
in this case, a side table or a stool, as well as a tray, using
the bar as a handle.

153

anonym (Deutschland) / anonymous (Germany)
Stuhl / chair
ca. 1810–1820
87,5 x 45 x 44 cm
Kirschbaumholz, massiv und furniert; Baumwolle; Leinen;
Rosshaar / cherry tree wood, massif and veneered; cotton;
linen; horsehair
Georg Böhringer Kunsthandel, Düsseldorf

Das vom Begründer der wissenschaftlichen Kunstge-
schichte, Johann Joachim Winckelmann, formulierte
Kunstideal der „edlen Einfalt und stillen Größe" findet in
diesem Biedermeier-Stuhl seinen Ausdruck im aufwändig
verarbeiteten, edlen Furnier und der schlichten Form, die
sich in ihrer Wirkung gegenseitig steigern.

Articulated by Johann Joachim Winckelmann, the founder
of the academic discipline of art history, the artistic idea
of "noble simplicity and quiet grandeur" is expressed
here in the careful craftsmanship of the elegant veneer
and simple form, which combine to achieve a mutually
enhancing effect.

154

Tischlampe / table lamp
Nr. 7344 (Variante des Modells / variation of model)
1928
Schwintzer & Gräff, Berlin
42 x 26,5 x 26,5 cm
vernickeltes Messing; Aluminium / nickel-plated brass;
aluminium
Collection Vitra Design Museum, Weil am Rhein

In den seriell produzierten Leuchten der Metallwerkstatt
des Bauhaus kommt die programmatische Zusammen-
führung von Kunst, Handwerk und moderner Technik
besonders gut zum Ausdruck. Die stellvertretende Leiterin
dieser Werkstatt, Marianne Brandt, hatte ein Exemplar
dieses (heute) anonymen Entwurfs auf dem Arbeitstisch
ihres Wohnateliers.

In the serially produced lamps of the Bauhaus metal-
working workshop, the programmatic unification of art,
craft, and modern technology is expressed in exemplary
fashion. The deputy head of the workshop, Marianne
Brandt, had a version of this (now) anonymous design on
her desk in the studio where she lived.

155

anonym / anonymous (USA)
Schaukelsessel / rocking chair
1876–80
Shaker Community, Mt. Lebanon, New York, NY
93,6 x 53 x 70,7 cm
Bugholz; Gurtbandgeflecht / bent wood; webbing-network
Collection Vitra Design Museum, Weil am Rhein

Zuverlässigkeit war für die Shaker eine moralische
Verpflichtung. Abgeschieden von den Neuerungen der
Zivilisation fand diese religiöse Gemeinschaft im 18.
und 19. Jahrhundert zu vereinfachten, funktionalisierten
und typisierten Formen ihrer Gebrauchsgegenstände,
die in höchster handwerklicher Perfektion äußerst stabil
gebaut wurden.

For the Shakers, reliability took on the importance of a
moral obligation. Isolated from the innovations of civili-
zation, this religious community of the eighteenth and
nineteenth centuries applied simplified, functionalized,
and standardized forms to their articles of daily use.
These were built to be exceptionally stable, fulfilling the
highest standards of craftsmanship.

156

Jean Prouvé
Stuhl / chair
482 (Standard)
1950
Ateliers Jean Prouvé, Nancy-Maxéville
79,9 x 42,7 x 48,2 cm
lackiertes Stahlblech; lackiertes Stahlrohr; Sperrholz /
lacquered sheet steel; lacquered tubular steel; plywood
Collection Vitra Design Musedum, Weil am Rhein

Jean Prouvé war Ingenieur, Industrieller und Designer,
ein Industriedesigner „par excellence". Bei diesem von
ihm selbst so genannten *Standard*-Stuhl – ein ebenso
preiswertes wie robustes Möbel, das er für die neu auf-
zubauenden Wohnungen und Einrichtungen im Nach-
kriegsfrankreich entwickelt hatte – handelt es sich um
einen Prototypen, also die Fassung eines Entwurfs, die
als Modell für die folgende Serienproduktion dient.

As an engineer, industrialist, and designer, Jean Prouvé
was an industrial designer *par excellence*. Developed
to provide inexpensive and durable furnishing for the
apartments and interiors being built in post-war France,
this version of the *Standard* chair, as he called it, was a
prototype and served as a model for subsequent serial
production.

157

Jasper Morrison
Stuhl / chair
Ply-Chair
1988
Vitra AG, Basel
84,5 x 39,5 x 47 cm
Multiplex-Profil, verleimt, mit Birkendeckfurnier /
cemented plywood section with birch face veneer
Collection Vitra Design Museum, Weil am Rhein

In diesem Stuhl – erstmals 1988 in Berlin als Teil seiner
Rauminstallation *Some New Items for the Home* vor-
gestellt – zeigt sich Jasper Morrisons Besinnung auf
wesentliche, unzweifelhafte Eigenschaften eines Gegen-
standes, die er aus der Geschichte seiner Formentwick-
lung zu destillieren versucht. Sein Ziel ist es, zu Objekten
zu finden, die im Alltagsleben vollständig aufgehen.

Presented for the first time in 1988 as part of his *Some
New Items for the Home* installation in Berlin, this chair

shows Jasper Morrison's reflections on the essential,
unquestioned characteristics of an object, distilled from
the historical development of its form. Morrison's goal
has always been to design objects that perfectly merge
into the fabric of everyday life.

158
Andrea Zittel
Skulptur / sculpture
A-Z Escape Vehicle, ZA 1997-002
1996/97
A-Z Enterprise, Brooklyn, NY
153 x 214 x 102 cm
verschiedene Materialien / mixed media
Collection Vitra Design Museum, Weil am Rhein

Andrea Zittels *Escape Vehicles* sind Refugien, um den
Störungen der Außenwelt zu entkommen: Auf kleinstem
Raum, den sich jeder Besitzer nach eigenen Vorstellungen
ausstatten soll, schaffen sie Platz für das innere Univer-
sum. Zwar macht ihre Leichtbauweise es möglich, sie
überall hin zu transportieren, doch im Grunde gelingt die
Flucht schon beim Betreten.

Andrea Zittel's *Escape Vehicles* serve as refuges that
allow one to get away from the disturbances of the
out-side world. In a highly compact space, to be outfitted
as the owner sees fit, they chart out a realm for
the inner universe. While their lightweight construction
allows them to be transported anywhere and everywhere,
escape is already assured just by stepping inside.

BILDNACHWEISE / ILLUSTRATION CREDITS

© Vitra Design Museum. Andreas Sütterlin, Fotos / photos: Abb. / ill. 1-6, S. / p. 6/7; Abb. / ill. 7-12, S. / p. 8/9; Abb. / ill. 13-19, S. / p. 10; Abb. / ill. 21-33, S. / p. 12/13; Abb. / ill. 36, S. / p. 14; Abb. / ill. 37, S. / p. 15; Abb. / ill. 38-55, S. / p. 40/41; Abb. / ill. 56-60, S. / p. 42/43; Abb. / ill. 61, 62, S. / p. 44/45; Abb. / ill. 66, S. / p. 47; Abb. / ill. 68-70, S. / p. 49; Abb. / ill. 71, S. / p. 50; Abb. / ill. 75, S. / p. 53; Abb. / ill. 76, 77, S. / p. 54; Abb. / ill. 80-82, S. / p. 66/67; Abb. / ill. 84, 85, S. / p. 68/69; Abb. / ill. 88, S. / p. 71; Abb. / ill. 92, S. / p. 74; Abb. / ill. 95, S. / p. 77; Abb. / ill. 97-99, S. / p. 84/85; Abb. / ill. 101, S. / p. 87; Abb. / ill. 103, S. / p. 88/89; Abb. / ill. 105, 106, S. / p. 90; Abb. / ill. 108, S. / p. 92; Abb. / ill. 112, S. / p. 93; Abb. / ill. 114, S. / p. 94; Abb. / ill. 118, S. / p. 95; Abb. / ill. 125-127, S. / p. 98/99; Abb. / ill. 129, S. / p. 100; Abb. / ill. 131, 134, S. / p. 101; Abb. / ill. 135, 136, S. / p. 102/103; Abb. / ill. 137-140, S. / p. 104-105; Abb. / ill. 145-147, S. / p. 109; Abb. / ill. 148, S. / p. 122; Abb. / ill. 151, S. / p. 124; Abb. / ill. 158, S. / p. 129.

© Toshiyuki Kita. Satoshi Akasawa, Foto / photo: Abb. / ill. 20, S. / p. 11.

© Hi-Cone. Felix Dobbert, Foto / photo: Abb. / ill. 34, S. / p. 13, S. / p. 80.

© Boghossian SA, Genève: Abb. / ill. 35, S. / p. 14.

© gta Archiv, ETH Zürich, Nachlass Hannes Meyer: S. / p. 22.

© Bibliothèque nationale de France: S. / p. 24.

© Royal Museums of Fine Arts of Belgium, Brussels: S. / p. 26.

© Vitra (www.vitra.com): S. / p. 27.

© The Cambridge Wittgenstein Archive: S. / p. 29.

© The Museum of Modern Art, New York / Scala, Florence, 2010 / © VG Bild-Kunst, Bonn 2010: S. / p. 32.

© Tate, London / © VG Bild-Kunst, Bonn 2010: S. / p. 34.

© Dr. Stephan Consemüller / © Bauhaus-Archiv Berlin: S. / p. 35.

© Robert Nachbargauer: S. / p. 36.

© Vitra Design Museum. Andreas Jung, Fotos / photos: Abb. / ill. 63, S. / p. 45; Abb. / ill. 67, S. / p. 48; Abb. / ill. 72, S. / p. 51; Abb. / ill. 90, S. / p. 73; Abb. / ill. 100, S. / p. 86; Abb. / ill. 104, S. / p. 89; Abb. / ill. 119, S. 96; Abb. / ill. 123, S. / p. 97; Abb. / ill. 154, S. / p. 125; Abb. / ill. 156, S. / p. 127.

© Vitra Design Museum. Thomas Dix, Fotos / photos: Abb. / ill. 65, S. / p. 46; Abb. / ill. 73, S. / p. 52; Abb. / ill. 74, S. / p. 52; Abb. / ill. 79, S. / p. 55; Abb. / ill. 83, S. / p. 67; Abb. / ill. 89, S. / p. 72; Abb. / ill. 93, S. / p. 75; Abb. / ill. 96, S. / p. 77; Abb. / ill. 102, S. / p. 87; Abb. / ill. 109, S. / p. 92; Abb. / ill. 110, S. / p. 93; Abb. / ill. 111, S. / p. 93; Abb. / ill. 115, S. 94; Abb. / ill. 122, S. / p. 97; Abb. / ill. 133, S. / p. 101; Abb. / ill. 144, S. / p. 108; Abb. / ill. 152, S. / p. 124; Abb. / ill. 157, S. / p. 128.

© Tata Motors Ltd., Mumbai: Abb. / ill. 86, S. / p. 69.

© Sebastian Jacobi. Felix Wirth, Fotos / photos: Abb. / ill. 91, S. / p. 73; Abb. / ill. 120, S. / p. 96; Abb. / ill. 128, S. / p. 99.

© Shigeru Ban. voile, Foto / photo: Vorderseite Cover / front cover; Abb. / ill. 94, S. / p. 76.

© Judd Foundation, New York, NY / Marfa, TX: Abb. / ill. 107, S. / p. 91.

© Vitra International. Hansjörg Walter, Foto / photo: Abb. / ill. 132, S. / p. 101.

© Sammlung Scharf-Gerstenberg, Staatliche Museen zu Berlin, Stiftung Preußischer Kulturbesitz / © VG Bild-Kunst, Bonn 2010: S. / p. 116.

© Westfälisches Schulmuseum, Dortmund: S. / p. 117 links / left.

© Fondation Le Corbusier: S. /. 67, Abb. / ill. 83; S. / p. 123.

© The Henry Dreyfuss Archive, Cooper-Hewitt, National Design Museum, New York: S. / p. 120.

© Georg Böhringer Kunsthandel, Düsseldorf: Abb. / ill. 153, S. / p. 124.

© Vitra Design Museum. Roland Engerisser, Foto / photo: Abb. / ill. 155, S. / p. 126.

© Thorsten Romanus, Foto / photo: Innenseite Cover / inside cover.

© Vitra Design Museum, Fotograf unbekannt / photographer unknown: Abb. / ill. 141, S. / p. 106; Abb. / ill. 149, S. / p. 122.

© VG Bild-Kunst, Bonn 2010: S. / p. 52 (Stiletto, Consumer's Rest); S. / p. 67 (Le Corbusier, für / for Pavillon du Brésil, Cité Internationale Universitaire, Paris); S. / p. 71 (Wilhelm Wagenfeld, Kubus); S. / p. 87 (Gerrit Rietveld, Roodblauwe stoel); S. / p. 91 (Donald Judd, No. 84/8, 1997); S. / p. 94 (Isamu Noguchi, IN-52); S. / p. 96 (Isamu Noguchi, Akari 120 A); S. 98 (Ludwig Mies van der Rohe, MR 50 (Brno)); S. / p. 99 (Ludwig Mies van der Rohe, MR 150/3); S. / p. 123 (Le Corbusier / C. Perriand, Fauteuil à dossier basculant); S. / p. 101 (Wilhelm Wagenfeld, Teeservice); S. / p. 105 (Jacques Le Chevallier, Chistera); S. / p. 109 (Gerrit Rietveld, Zig zag); S. / p. 124 (Walter Gropius, Türklinke); S. / p. 124 (Max Bill, Hocker).

© Succession Marcel Duchamp: S. / p. 32.

© The Isamu Noguchi Foundation and Garden Museum: S. / p. 94 / Abb. / ill. 115; S. / p. 96; Abb. / ill. 119.

© 2010 Secretariat und Bühnen Archiv Oskar Schlemmer, IT - 28824 Oggebbio (VB), www.schlemmer.org: S. / p. 118.

> JAPANESE GUESTHOUSE
Kyakuden
1863 / 2008
Domaine de Boisbuchet, Lessac-Confolens

>> Faustkeil / hand axe
Altsteinzeit / Palaèolithic
Collection Strüker, Basel
→ Abb. / ill. 47, S. / p. 17

DESIGN ≠ ART

DESIGN ≠ ART

FUNCTIONAL OBJECTS FROM DONALD JUDD
TO RACHEL WHITEREAD

BARBARA BLOEMINK

CURATORIAL DIRECTOR, COOPER-HEWITT, NATIONAL DESIGN MUSEUM

JOSEPH CUNNINGHAM

INDEPENDENT CURATOR

Smithsonian
Cooper-Hewitt, National Design Museum

MERRELL

R.A.C.C. Library

No   P16289

No   745·4442 BLO

05 OCT 2005

When establishing the first design museum in the United States at the Cooper Union in 1897, Eleanor, Amy, and Sarah Hewitt included paintings by Winslow Homer and Frederic Church alongside historic porcelain and silverware. They chose to include works of contemporary fine art alongside the "useful" decorative arts of the past in order to create a study collection for craftsmen and designers, noting, "For the worker, the source of inspiration is frequently found in the sight of an unexpected object, possibly one of an entirely different trade."

As Barbara Bloemink, Cooper-Hewitt's Curatorial Director and *Design ≠ Art* co-curator, reminds us in the opening essay to this book, the relationship between the fine and applied arts has been both harmonious and fractious. Despite the aspirations of the Hewitt sisters and countless proselytizers before them, modern Western society has found it necessary to distinguish between aesthetics and function: between the spiritual in art, and the corporeal in design. David Hockney's witheringly witty comment resonates in our ears: "Art has to move you and design does not, unless it's a good design for a bus."

Today, design is among the most accessible forms of visual culture, and *Design ≠ Art* brings together a number of issues that are particularly relevant for the National Design Museum at this time. The public "unveiling" of previously unknown design works by some of the most significant artists of the last forty years encourages us to explore the very nature of both design and art, and how one may distinguish between the two. These questions are not new; however, the increasing visibility and importance given to design today allow us to confront the issue directly, even controversially, at a time when the definition of design itself is expanding to encompass myriad aspects of human creativity. By straightforwardly inserting the mathematical symbol ≠, defined as "not equal to, but not greater than and not less than," Cooper-Hewitt means to explore the boundaries and debates of the twentieth-century art world, as it sought to define, divide, or conflate its expressions in a world of increasing mass consumption, mass media, and popular culture.

01. Mrs. Andrew Carnegie's bedroom, 1938

Design ≠ Art quite consciously follows on from Cooper-Hewitt's preceding exhibition, *Shock of the Old: Christopher Dresser*. Dr. Dresser presented a wholeheartedly Victorian world view, in which science, art, and industry were united. *Design ≠ Art* presents an altogether more complicated, and rich, view of life and artistic output.

The exhibition consciously undercuts our art-historical preconceptions by conducting this exploration within the Andrew Carnegie mansion, home of Cooper-Hewitt. Works by Donald Judd, Richard Tuttle, and Rosemarie Trockel, more usually placed within vast industrial vistas, are wryly arranged within the ornate grandeur of Mrs. Carnegie's former bedroom and dressing room—functional rooms that are a far cry from the "unmediated" experience traditionally called for by Minimalist art.

Design ≠ Art was conceived by Barbara Bloemink, who has explored the boundaries of artistic expression and media in photography, theater-set design, and the decorative arts throughout her career. She and co-curator Joseph Cunningham have brought together an astonishing group of design objects, most of which are being seen in a museum context for the first time in *Design ≠ Art*. I thank both Barbara and Joe very much indeed for this remarkable book and exhibition.

Special thanks are also due to Cooper-Hewitt Trustee Barbara Mandel and her husband Morton, who have generously supported this exhibition, book, and attendant conference. Barbara and Mort's deep love and knowledge of Minimalism and post-Minimalism are manifest in their extraordinary collection of art, and I thank them for helping Cooper-Hewitt introduce the unexplored design facet of these artists' careers to the general public.

The exhibition itself was greatly enhanced through the efforts of the collectors, museums, and galleries who have agreed to lend works and images. In particular, we are grateful to Richard Tuttle, Madeleine Hoffmann and Rainer Judd of the Judd Foundation; Elisabeth Cunnick of A/D Gallery; and Max Protetch of the Max Protetch Gallery. We also thank Peter Ballantine, Randy Sanchez, Craig Rember, and the Board of Trustees of the Judd Foundation; Josie Browne, Stuart Krimko, and Chris Davison of Max Protetch Gallery; Paul Walter; James Zemaitis of Sotheby's; Angela Westwater of Sperone Westwater; Susanna Singer; Bonnie Rychlak, Amy Hau, and Carl Riddle of the Noguchi Foundation; Brooke Alexander and Owen Houhoulis of Brooke Alexander Gallery; Noah Khoshbin, Curator, Robert Wilson Gallery; Angelo Benini of Ten Coconuts; Lindsay Walt; Sheri Pasquarelli, Director, and Jay Gorney, Partner, Gorney Bravin + Lee Gallery; Bill Ehrlich and Jane Fire of Artes Magnus; Jeffrey Lee of Mary Ryan Gallery; Steven Berger; Maureen Sarro of Friedrich Petzel Gallery; Nicholas Sands; Lewis Nerman; Katherine Chan of Nolan/Eckman Gallery; Dwight Hackett of Dwight Hackett Projects; Sarah Nichols, Elizabeth Agro, and Richard Armstrong of the Carnegie Museum of Art; Jaime Frankfurt; Barbara Goldfarb; Petra Singh of Petra Singh Equator Studios; Kiki Smith; Jim Dicke II; Barbara Schröder of the Dia Art Foundation; Michael Wolleager, Editor-in-Chief, and Vanessa Kogevinas, Associate Editor, of *Western Interiors and Design* magazine; Paul Franklin and Dan Gimenez of *nest* magazine; Lisa Eisner; Dudley del Balso; Dean Sobel, Director of the Aspen Art Museum; Joseph Holtzman; Urs Fischer; Steven Beyer; John Smith of The Andy Warhol Museum; and Flavin Judd.

   In addition, neither the book nor the exhibition would have been possible without the extraordinary efforts of a number of Cooper-Hewitt staff. Museum editor Chul R. Kim and curatorial assistants Allison Harbertson and Elizabeth Chase put in countless hours, conducting research, editing the texts, organizing the images, loans, and timeline information, and managing the myriad details involved. Registrar Steven Langehough, head of exhibitions Jocelyn Groom, and graduate interns Wava Carpenter and Fawn Ellis assisted greatly in bringing this project to fruition. Thanks are also due to Sandra Wheeler and Alfred Zollinger of Matter Practice; Catarina Tsang, Patrick Seymour, and Matthew Pimm of Tsang Seymour Design; Anita Jorgensen Lighting Design; Alicia Cheng and Sarah Gephart of mgmt.; and Hugh Merrell, Julian Honer, Anthea Snow, Nicola Bailey, and Michelle Draycott of Merrell Publishers.

Finally, we are profoundly grateful to the artists, whose response to this exhibition has been overwhelmingly enthusiastic. Many among them have been eager for the opportunity to share with the world their design works, as well as their thoughts on the borderlines that lie within their work. The curators and I wish to offer our sincere thanks to them, their families, and their colleagues for their extraordinary generosity and support.

Donald Judd, installation view, *Donald Judd Furniture – Retrospective*, Museum Villa Stuck, Munich, Germany, 1993

Rachel Whiteread, installation view, *Daybed*,
A/D Gallery, New York, 2000

ON THE RELATIONSHIP OF ART AND DESIGN

BARBARA BLOEMINK

02. Donald Judd, interior view, Bank building, Marfa, TX

03. Michelangelo Buonarroti, candelabrum, *c.* 1530–40. Black chalk, brush and brown wash, incised lines, and compass marks on cream laid paper, lined

INTRODUCTION: SAMENESS AND DIFFERENCE

IS THERE A DIFFERENCE BETWEEN ART AND DESIGN?

As distinctions among many previously discrete concepts become increasingly ambiguous, it is an appropriate time to reconsider the traditionally held differences between the two.[1] Although the discussion is not a new one, the current ascendance of design gives renewed relevance to questions concerning the validity of art's conventionally privileged position. The visibility, market value, and wide-ranging interest in design today offer an opportunity to examine how, particularly in the twentieth century, these confining definitions resulted in a tendency to view artists and designers from a single perspective, and to overlook work that did not fit neatly within distinct categories. Perhaps, as with the emperor's new clothes, it is time to step back and consider: hasn't art always had a function? Isn't there usually artistry in design? It is the contradiction and inherent truth of this duality—that design and art are simultaneously both different and the same—that enable us to gain a new perspective on, and insight into, both, and to discover previously "invisible" work that falls somewhere in between.

In 1962, as the first works of art later termed "Minimalist" were being developed, art historian George Kubler opened his seminal book, *The Shape of Time,* with this statement: "Let us suppose that the idea of art can be expanded to embrace the whole range of man-made things. . . . By this view, the universe of man-made things simply coincides with the history of art."[2] Observing that nothing is made unless it is desirable, Kubler condemned our clumsy tendency to segregate art from functional work, as in doing so we risked ignoring a great deal of subtle variation, complexity, and divergent examples, as well as rival systems of thought and production. He therefore urged that we "view the processes common to both art and science in the same historical perspective." Maintaining it was unlikely that many significant artists remained undiscovered, he suggested instead that by examining the past with an open mind, "unfamiliar types of artistic effort" would be revealed.[3]

Among the little-known forms of artistic effort currently making what is, in many cases, their first public appearance are the functional designs from the late 1960s to today made by the artists featured in *Design ≠ Art.* Unknown to most admirers of their work, many of the so-called "Minimalist" and "post-Minimalist" artists also produced a significant amount of furniture and design. Until recently, these works have been largely unacknowledged by these artists and the galleries that show their art. The present emergence of this work represents both an expression of the renewed interest in design and an admission of the invalidity of past attempts to categorize these artists through only one aspect of their œuvre.

The separation of "fine" art from design is a fairly recent Western conceit, and has only been considered an issue during certain eras. So too is the idea, still prevalent, that art is "non-functional." Throughout Western history, art has functioned as religious, ideological, and political propaganda, economic currency, commodity, decoration, and as a vehicle for personal self-aggrandizement. The historical delimitation of art and design has often been imprecise, resulting in greater or lesser congruence. As a result, a surprising number of individuals from the past whom we identify today primarily as artists also gained acclaim for their functional designs. It is worth considering a few examples to put the objects discussed in this book in context.

As Arthur C. Danto has observed, by the Renaissance, as painters and sculptors lost their anonymity and became identified by name, "the beautiful and the practical were as much an undifferentiated unity as are, in philosophical truth, the body and the mind."[4] A number of Renaissance painters, including Raphael, Botticelli, and Michelangelo, practiced functional and decorative arts. In addition to his various architectural projects, paintings, and sculpture, Michelangelo, for example, also designed functional objects including a salt cellar, an altar table, and an elaborate candelabrum (fig. 03).

The practice of working comfortably in both art and design continued among many artists throughout the following centuries. Although best known for his engravings, the Italian artist Giovanni Battista Piranesi also designed architecture, stage sets, and furniture. In his treatise of 1769, *Diverse maniere d'adornare i cammini ed ogni altra parte degli edifizi,* Piranesi promoted the need for a modern style of interior design based on eclectic, and often antique, sources.[5] In addition to designing over sixty ornamental chimney-pieces, Piranesi made drawings for over one hundred items of furniture, including chairs, coaches, commodes, and clocks (fig. 04).

During the eighteenth century, there were also very close stylistic correlations in painting, sculpture, and the decorative arts throughout the European royal

04

05

04. Giovanni Battista Piranesi, commode with a clock flanked by two vases, 1769. Etching

05. John Singleton Copley, *Sarah Erving Waldo, c.* 1765. Oil on canvas

06. Henri Cartier-Bresson, photograph of Henri Matisse, *c.* 1943–44

06

courts. In France, for example, the Rococo arabesques in Jean-Antoine Watteau's paintings were echoed in the furniture and ormolu designs of noted *ébéniste* Charles Cressent. Hubert Robert, who gained renown as a court painter for Louis XVI, designed a set of Jacob chairs "*de forme nouvelle de genre étrusque*" ("in a new form of the Etruscan genre"), and a pair of regal, austere thrones for Marie Antoinette's Neo-classical dairy at the Château de Rambouillet, near Versailles. In Britain and the United States, the stylistic parallels between the fine and decorative arts were readily apparent in portraits by such artists as John Trumbull, John Singleton Copley, and Thomas Gainsborough. These paintings all portray stylistic affinities, from the dress of the sitter to the realistic depictions of adjacent design objects, such as furniture, that complete the settings (fig. 05).

By the latter part of the eighteenth century, however, "fine" art and the decorative arts in Europe became increasingly segregated. Government-sponsored art academies began to position painting and sculpture as the highest form of art, defined as "sources of aesthetic pleasure uncontaminated by the squalor of practicality."[6] This distancing of the so-called "fine" arts from functional design continued through much of the nineteenth century, and it was rare for designers to achieve parity in recognition, reputation, and financial reward with their artist contemporaries.

The renewed status of the decorative arts in France at the end of the nineteenth century was due, in part, to economics. Realizing that the nation's population growth was not keeping pace with that of Germany, the French government actively sanctioned the Art Nouveau movement. It hoped that the latter, with its organic and decorative-arts focus, would bring French women interested in the emergent women's liberation movement back into the domestic environment. The government also established an annual Salon for the decorative arts, so that they were accorded the same prestige and academic status as the fine arts.[7] The burgeoning middle classes, however, increasingly collected and used painting and sculpture as status symbols, reflecting their intellectual and cultural prowess. In *Notes of a Painter* (1908), Henri Matisse (fig. 06) compared art's cerebral, transformative powers to the physical comforts of a good armchair: "What I dream of is an art of balance, of purity and serenity devoid of any troubling or depressing subject matter, an art which might be for every cerebral worker, be he businessman or writer, like an appeasing influence, like a mental soother, something like a good armchair in which to rest from physical fatigue."[8]

In 1912, the French sculptor Raymond Duchamp-Villon decided the modern era needed a new architectural setting in which the decorative arts would be integrated with, and considered equal to, the fine arts. At that year's Paris Salon des Beaux-Arts, he designed a geometrically ornamented plaster façade, through which visitors entered into what became known as the Maison Cubiste. The "house" consisted of three rooms painted in primary colors. In each room, paintings coexisted as part of a decorative scheme with wall moldings, fireplace designs, mantle clocks, and other functional objects, including chandeliers by Duchamp-Villon, a tea service for six designed by his brother Jacques Villon, and mirrors with inset paintings by Marie Laurencin.[9] Although the design of the rooms did not conform to our contemporary notions of "Cubist" style, they were considered extremely innovative for promoting a less expensive, more diverse "style" than traditional interiors, which required stylistic unity.

During the period between the two World Wars, a number of artists in Europe and the United States rejected historical definitions and subjects for art, turning instead to pure, primary, abstract forms. Later, in a 1965 article on the burgeoning geometric, minimal aesthetic of many young artists including Donald Judd, art historian Barbara Rose noted two precedents for their radical, reductivist style: "On the eve of the First World War, two artists—one in Moscow, Kasimir Malevich, and the other in Paris, Marcel Duchamp—made decisions that radically altered the course of art history."[10] As Rose rightly suggested, it is difficult to understand what came to be known as Minimalism without exploring the Dada work of Marcel Duchamp and the aesthetics and philosophy underlying the work of the Russian Constructivists.

In the early decades of the twentieth century, Duchamp grew disaffected with the auteur aspects and the subject matter of contemporary painting and sculpture. At the same time, he became very interested in industrial products that offered viewers "the beauty of indifference," particularly objects with a design that was not based on any form of narrative. In 1913, he took a commercial bicycle wheel, mounted it on a kitchen stool, and declared it art. He also purchased a commercial bottle rack, which he signed, thereby creating the first

07

08

07. Marcel Duchamp, *Bottle Rack,* 1914. Steel

08. Marcel Duchamp's *In Advance of the Broken Arm* (original 1915) at Donald Judd's Spring Street studio, New York

works in a series he titled *Ready-mades* (fig. 07). Along with his *In Advance of the Broken Arm* (a commercial snow shovel hung on the wall), and his infamous *Fountain* (a mass-produced urinal), Duchamp used these ordinary objects to investigate and question traditional definitions of "art." As he later wrote, "The choices of these *Ready-mades* were based on a reaction of visual indifference with at the same time a total absence of good or bad taste. . . . Another aspect of the *Ready-made* is its lack of uniqueness . . . in fact nearly every one of the *Ready-mades* existing today is not an original in the conventional sense."[11]

By rejecting uniqueness as a defining quality for works of art and displaying mass-produced objects as sculpture, Duchamp abandoned the necessity of the artist's hand in making the work. As Rosalind Krauss has noted, "His work is not intended to hold the object up for examination, but to scrutinize the act of aesthetic transformation itself."[12] Duchamp's influence was central to the work of a number of the Minimalist artists. Donald Judd's library in Marfa, Texas, contains a wide variety of books on the French artist's work, and he hung a version of Duchamp's *In Advance of the Broken Arm* on the wall of his Spring Street home in New York City, around the corner from the bedrooms (fig. 08).[13] In a particularly Duchampian twist, Judd also purchased and hung a commercial bottle rack on the wall of his son's room at Spring Street, ironically commenting on Duchamp's *Bottle Rack*. The French provocateur also influenced many of the Minimalist artists, such as Dan Flavin and Richard Tuttle, who used found objects in their works of art.

In Russia, the brief, but highly influential, Constructivist movement emerged after the 1917 Revolution and lasted until 1922. Avoiding "elitist" subject matter, iconography, and materials, the Constructivist artists espoused a new ideology that dissolved distinctions between art, design, and architecture. Using terminology that anticipated Minimalism, the Constructivists rejected ornamentation. They defined the fundamentals of their new style of stylistically geometric, abstract forms with a limited color palette; simple, impersonal materials that were easily found and inexpensive; and engineering techniques in place of the individual artist's gesture. Vladimir Tatlin, for example, abandoned traditional artists' techniques and adopted industrial materials, including metal and plastic, in his work. He insisted that "the artist must become a technician" and learn the tools and materials of modern production in order to benefit the proletariat. Among other things, he devised variants of an oven that combined maximum heat output with minimum fuel consumption. Dan Flavin would later title one of his light-works of 1964 *Homage to Vladimir Tatlin*, indicating his admiration for the Russian avant-garde artist's work.

Even within the Russian avant garde, however, individual artists held different views. Wassily Kandinsky and Kasimir Malevich believed that art was essentially a *spiritual* endeavor, and therefore conspicuously non-useful. Nevertheless, despite believing that industrial design was a secondary activity, after spending time under the influence of the Bauhaus in Munich, Kandinsky designed a porcelain tea service in 1923. Its painted motifs are similar to those in his painting of the same year, *Circles in Black*. Kandinsky soon designed another porcelain service, produced by the Petrograd Porcelain Factory, for the first Russian exhibition at the Galeries van Diemen in Berlin (fig. 09).[14]

Aleksandr Rodchenko was a far more politically oriented artist than Kandinsky. An avowed Communist, Rodchenko abandoned painting in 1921 in order to devote all of his work to the Russian Revolution. Like many of his fellow Constructivists, Rodchenko wanted to transform every aspect of life, designing

09

09. Wassily Kandinsky, *Suprematist Cup and Saucer*, 1923. Porcelain

10. Aleksandr Rodchenko, *Workers' Club*, installation at the 1925 *Exposition Internationale des Arts Décoratifs et Industriels Modernes*, Paris

10

a perpetual-motion machine, posters, candy wrappers, furniture, and teapots to suit the Revolution's theoretical construct. In 1925, he designed the *Workers' Club,* which was installed at the Russian pavilion of the *Exposition Internationale des Arts Décoratifs et Industriels Modernes* in Paris (fig. 10). The *Workers' Club* was widely seen and publicized as an interior specifically created to serve as a center of daily life, amusement, and political activities. Its design was based on two main principles: economy of space and maximum flexible usage. The furniture, for example, was made of strictly rectilinear, geometric forms, using simple materials and visible joints, with the intention that it could be produced all over the Soviet Union.[15]

During the first few decades of the twentieth century, various loosely defined groups of artists throughout Europe and America included decorative arts and design as an integral part of their defining philosophy. Around 1917, for example, painters Piet Mondrian, Robert Delaunay, and Theo van Doesburg joined with sculptor Georges Vantongerloo and designer Gerrit Rietveld to found a magazine entitled *De Stijl,* which was first published in The Netherlands and quickly circulated throughout Europe. Their aim was to disseminate their new stylistic aesthetic in which "above all else, truth, function, and construction are expressed. [De Stijl] comprises all problems of detail, construction, creativity, and economics."[16] Based on the fundamentals of limited primary colors (plus black and white), rectangular lines, space, and simple forms, their work was intended to have no reference to the representational, concrete world.

Issues of *De Stijl* magazine often included features on the work of the Russian Constructivists. Following their lead, the artists similarly engaged design to expand their aesthetic theories to encompass every aspect of daily life. Sonia Delaunay, for example, gave as much attention to the design of furniture and clothing as she did to her painting. In the 1920s, she worked with Dada propagandist Tristan Tzara on "poem-dresses," and her apartment in Paris became a fashion studio where, some claim, she introduced the concept of *prêt-à-porter* clothing. Throughout her career, Delaunay designed cushion covers, lampshades, glasses, curtains, and furniture, including a sycamore commode in 1924. Like many European artists of the time, Delaunay also designed costumes and sets for various theatrical productions, including Diaghilev's *Ballets Russes.*

In 1919, the German architect Walter Gropius founded the Bauhaus school and movement in order to "coordinate all creative effort, to achieve, in a new architecture, the unification of all training in art and design." Acknowledging the complexity of designing functional objects, Ludwig Mies van der Rohe later noted, "A chair is a very difficult object. A skyscraper is almost easier. That is why Chippendale is so famous."[17] In addition to architects Marcel Breuer and Mies van der Rohe, Bauhaus instructors included the painters Paul Klee and Josef Albers. Although known primarily for his serial paintings, Albers also designed furniture, tea glasses, wallpaper, glass windows, and record covers. A number of Albers's furniture designs appear to be direct precedents for those of the artists working with the tenets of Minimalism several decades later. Donald Judd, for example, was not only aware of Albers's work, he was among the first art critics to review and promote Albers's painting, writings, and philosophy on color interaction in the early 1960s. Judd maintained a great respect for Albers's work throughout his life.[18]

The interest in abstraction and the furthering of a visual language of pure and simple primary forms continued intermittently throughout the 1940s, often coinciding with more organic and increasingly emotionally and politically based art. Constantin Brancusi's work, for example, although often figurative in its titles, is often cited by the artists associated with Minimalism as a primary influence. In addition to extraordinary sculpture in metal, stone, and wood, Brancusi designed and crafted abstract stands as furniture-bases for his sculpture. The artist considered these pedestals integral to the final works. Like so many of the artists who followed him in working with simple materials and minimal forms, Brancusi was particularly interested in the relationship between his work and the architectural context.

Isamu Noguchi, the Japanese-American artist, was apprenticed to Brancusi in Paris before returning to New York and developing his own vocabulary of forms. Throughout his career, Noguchi continually experimented with the opposing styles of geometric abstraction and biomorphism, and with the dialogue among works of art, design, and their architectural context. As he often stated, "Everything is sculpture, any materials, any idea without hindrance born into space, I consider sculpture." Presaging Scott Burton's work, Noguchi aspired to make sculpture useful and integrated into everyday life (fig. 11). Designing

11. Isamu Noguchi, *Alcoa Forecast Program Tables*, 1957. Aluminum and paint

12. Isamu Noguchi, prototype of *Akari #33N Model Floor Lamp*, 1951. Handmade washi paper and bamboo ribbing, electrical fixture

13

14

13. Meret Oppenheim, *Table aux pieds d'oiseau*, 1939, editioned by Oppenheim in 1983. Wood, gold leaf, and brass

14. Yves Klein, *Table*, 1961. International Klein blue pigment, glass, Plexiglas, and steel

monumental sculpture as outdoor public art became an important element of his later work from the 1950s through the 1980s.

Noguchi's range was prodigious: he simultaneously worked as a sculptor, draftsman, potter, product and furniture designer, architect, landscape architect, and stage designer. In 1939, he designed his first piece of furniture, a low glass-topped table, with biomorphic wooden legs. Noguchi designed furniture throughout the 1940s, and a number of his designs were put into production by Herman Miller, Inc. During this decade, he also made lighting fixtures that he titled *Lunars.* While in Japan in the early 1950s, Noguchi designed his first *Akari* lamps using traditional mulberry-bark paper and bamboo. The artist saw these lamps as both functional lighting sources and sculptures, and designed a great variety of shapes and sizes. By using inexpensive materials and traditions of working, Noguchi sought to make his *Akari* lamps available to a large number of people. By the mid-1950s, the *Akari* lamps were widely exported, and they are still in production (fig. 12). In all of his work, Noguchi saw his task as shaping space, in the sense that he believed art should "disappear" into its surroundings with a sense of oneness.

A number of notable twentieth-century artists experimented with both furniture and design. In Europe, Dada and Surrealist artists frequently combined found objects with incongruous materials in a surprising, and often disconcerting, manner. Meret Oppenheim's infamous fur-lined teacup and saucer, *Object* (1936), confounded viewers with its bizarre juxtaposition of materials and dysfunctionality. Three years later, Oppenheim designed a table with a circular top, held up by two legs. Rather than having plain straight supports to echo stylistically the simple tabletop, the object's limbs terminated in the feet of a claw-toed bird (fig. 13). Many other artists, including Pablo Picasso, worked in clay, creating functional ceramics that were mainly extensions of the visual iconography of their artworks. Other artists, including Alexander Calder, designed wearable sculpture and children's toys.

In 1961, French artist Yves Klein made a series of tables in which he "floated" his characteristic blue and rose pigments and gold leaf within individual Plexiglas boxes (fig. 14). Klein was particularly interested in the idea of the infinite—which he called "the Void"—and used monochromatic colors to fill the interior space of the thin, rectangular boxes. Philosophically, Klein believed in the "raw ground of being, the underlying reality of 'is-ness' that unites all things and obliterates their surface differences."[19] Commenting in 1963 on Klein's work, Judd offered his ultimate praise, noting that the artist's paintings were "simple and broadly scaled, they tend to become objects and consequently, they have a new intensity. . . . Yves Klein's blue paintings are the only ones that are unspatial."[20]

While living in Paris in 1951, Judd's contemporary, the painter Ellsworth Kelly, designed a nine-panel folding screen, the design of which replicates the rhythm made by the shadow of a railing falling across the metal staircase in La Combe, a villa outside Paris (fig. 15). This was one of many works of the early 1950s in which Kelly explored the effects of light and shadow. In 1957, he extended the screen format, designing a series of proposals for corporate commissions. Kelly's *The Seven Sculptural Screens in Brass* was eventually installed at the Post House Restaurant in the Transportation Building at Penn Center in Philadelphia. During the 1960s, along with Andy Warhol and Chuck Close, Kelly was commissioned to design a rug based on his paintings. Kelly is adamant, however, that his *Primary Tapestry*, as he titled this work (fig. 16), be considered as a work of art and not as a rug. As he states:

> I don't consider *Primary Tapestry* functional or furniture/design as I would prefer it hang on the wall. I prefer to think of it as a work of art, and gave it a number in my archive similar to all of my other works of art. I don't differentiate between my tapestry and my art works; it is just a work of art in another material. I don't want any work of mine to be useful in any other way than to be looked at as a work of art. Because my work is largely made up of simple shapes and minimal qualities, it can too easily be slid into being superficially considered "decoration."[21]

This pejorative attitude toward design as superficial "decoration" remained prevalent throughout the 1960s and into the 1980s. As a result, many artists did not publicly acknowledge or exhibit their more functional, pragmatic furniture and design objects *unless* they were incorporated as part of an artwork or installation.

During the 1950s and 1960s, Robert Rauschenberg, reflecting the influence of Duchamp, rejected the idea that only selected materials were appropriate to art.

15. Ellsworth Kelly, *La Combe II*, 1950–51. Oil on wood, folding screen of nine hinged panels

16. Ellsworth Kelly, *Primary Tapestry*, 1967–68. Wool

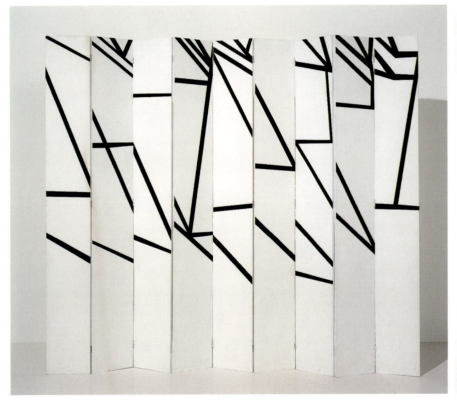

15

16

Instead, he mixed painting, collage, and actual objects into so-called "combines" (fig. 18). In these works, Rauschenberg often included mattresses, chairs, road signs, Coke bottles, blankets, and stuffed animals, fixed or inserted on to painted surfaces. Through the "combines," Rauschenberg was able to elicit viewers' questioning of the difference between a bed with blankets and pillow on a wall, versus when they are placed on the ground; and how re-situating items as art changes our perceptions of them. The artist also designed several functional objects, including water tables, a suite of cardboard furniture, and his *Tire Lamp* (fig. 17). These works balance the simple, direct materials of Minimalism with Duchamp's and the Dadaists' ironic humor and interplay of everyday objects and art. Judd was very taken with Rauschenberg's aesthetic and materials. In his 1962 review of Rauschenberg's work for *Arts Magazine,* Judd noted its unique qualities, particularly citing "the unrectangular and unflat format, the use of

17. Robert Rauschenberg, *Tire Lamp*, 1971. Tire, light bulbs, steel, and electrical fixture

18. Robert Rauschenberg, *Hog Heaven*, 1978. Solvent transfer on fabric collaged to wooden panels with acrylic paint, truck tire with collage, and wooden plank

19. Claes Oldenburg, *Leopard Chair*, 1963. Vinyl, wood, foam rubber, and metal

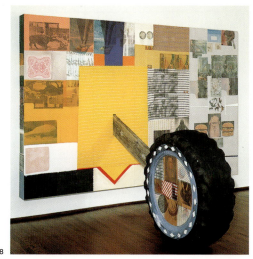
18

19

found and simply existing materials, and the casualness [that] are three of Rauschenberg's radical aspects."[22]

Pop artist Claes Oldenburg, despite his non-Minimalist tendencies, was also admired and written about by Judd. In 1963, recalling a motel room in Malibu, California, that he had seen as a child, Oldenburg began a series of sculptures related to domestic environments. The first prototype was a large, angular chair, covered with vinyl imitation-leopardskin material. The *Leopard Chair* was built by commercial manufacturers and constructed to slant at an oblique angle, giving it an exaggerated illusion of depth (fig. 19). The chair, like the other elements of his subsequent *Bedroom Ensemble,* resembles furniture, but according to the artist they are "pseudo-functionalist . . . like they were meant to be enjoyed or to be seen rather than used."[23]

An important break between art and design in the twentieth century accompanied the emergence of Abstract Expressionism, and its emphasis on pure painting, the individual, hand-wrought gesture of making, and the personal psychological expression of the artist. As early as 1947, in a catalogue essay for the *Ideographic Picture* exhibition, Abstract Expressionist Barnett Newman attacked what he termed the "meaningless materialism of design," thereby distancing his and his colleagues' gestural, painterly work from the decorative or applied arts.

In April 1966, The Jewish Museum in New York opened an exhibition titled *Primary Structures: Younger American and British Sculpture.* Although it featured artists of various contemporary aesthetic styles, the exhibition is also considered to have caused the first widespread awareness of early Minimalist art. *Primary Structures* introduced work by previously unknown artists, including Donald Judd, Sol LeWitt, Ellsworth Kelly, Dan Flavin, and Richard Artschwager. Sol LeWitt came up with the name "primary structures" to distinguish these three-dimensional artworks from traditional painting and sculpture media (figs. 20, 21).

Primary Structures and other early exhibitions featuring these artists received a great deal of attention. Many critics cited the new works' alliance with architecture, and considered their fundamental explorations of space, volume, movement, and light to be "concepts that are at the very heart of the most advanced thinking about modern architecture."[24] In his review in *The New Yorker*, Robert Coates praised the work, observing that in order to deal with the larger scale of this new form of art, the artists had begun "to function primarily as designer[s], making a scale model of the figure or construction and turning it over . . . to the lathe and milling machine operators, the welders, the foundry men . . . who will put together the sculpture."[25]

The polarization of the individualized, gestural Abstract Expressionist painting and the anonymously manufactured objects of the Minimalist artists was furthered in 1967 when Clement Greenberg, the most outspoken art critic of the time, celebrated Abstract Expressionism in his essay "The Recentness of Sculpture." Greenberg declared Abstract Expressionism to be the "true" innovative art form, as it was based on the artist's subjectivity and handiwork. He then denigrated the new Minimalist art, describing it as "closer to furniture than art," and claiming that it lacked formal complexity and feeling and was nothing more than a kind of "good design" that was preplanned and executed by someone else.[26]

Greenberg's essay, with its disparaging references to design, was published at around the same time as the initial forays into furniture by a number of the Minimalist artists. It therefore likely contributed to some of the artists' vehement declarations of differentiation between their art and design work, and to the concealment and downplay of their functional works in deference to their works of art. Although from the late 1960s through the following two decades, such artists as Judd, Chamberlain, Flavin, and LeWitt continued to design and manufacture furniture and design objects, these were rarely exposed to public scrutiny in gallery or museum exhibitions. Instead, the work remained largely under the radar of public consciousness.

Although problematic, the terms "Minimalism"[27] and "post-Minimalism" are so commonly used today that it is virtually impossible to discuss much of the work of the last four decades without using them. It is important to note, however, that not one of the artists whose work is associated with these terms accepted the labels. As Sol LeWitt observed, no one ever clearly defined Minimalism or put any limits on what it was: "Therefore I conclude that it is part of a secret language that art critics use when communicating with each other."[28] Most of the artists remained highly critical of having these terms used in relation to their work, and of any implication they carry of "reduction." As Donald Judd argued, "I object to the whole reduction idea, because it is only reduction of those things someone

20

21

20. Installation view, *Primary Structures* exhibition, The Jewish Museum, New York, 1966. Back left: Ellsworth Kelly, *Blue Disk*, 1963; center: Forrest Myer, *Zigarat*, 1966; back right: Dan Flavin, *Corner Monument 4*, c. 1966

21. Installation view, *Primary Structures* exhibition, The Jewish Museum, New York, 1966. Left to right: Robert Morris, *Untitled (two L-beams)*; Donald Judd, *Untitled*, 1966, and *Untitled*, 1966; Robert Grosvenor, *Transoxiana*, 1965

doesn't want. If my work is reductionist it's because it doesn't have the elements that people thought should be there. But it has other elements that I like."[29]

Instead of being defined styles or coherent movements, Minimalism and post-Minimalism reflect an often contentious dialogue among a number of highly idiosyncratic artists. Each held distinct, and occasionally opposing, viewpoints of how their work should be defined. In using these terms, one should keep in mind George Kubler's observation: "Style is like a rainbow. It is a phenomenon of perception governed by the coincidence of certain physical conditions. We see it only briefly while we pause between the sun and the rain, and it vanishes when we go to the place where we thought we saw it."[30]

All of the artists in *Design ≠ Art* have some relation to Minimalist tendencies in both their art and their design work. Their designs for furniture and functional objects grew, to one degree or another, out of shared ideas about form, space, and the role of the viewer generated through their art. These include an emphasis on the use of simple, geometric, often mass-produced materials and the elimination of detail, narrative, emotion, and subject matter. One of the things that make examining the functional objects made by the artists in *Design ≠ Art* so interesting is that, from the late 1960s, two contemporary artists, Donald Judd and Scott Burton, publicly posited completely contradictory, polar views on how design and art should be considered and defined. At virtually the same time that Judd laid down his thesis declaring the inherent differences between art and design, Burton announced his antithetical view that all future works of art should also function as pragmatic structures. The design work of many of their contemporaries falls somewhere within the continuum between these two extreme positions.

By contrast, Richard Tuttle deliberately problematizes distinctions between art and design. Synthesizing principles from each, he considers them both as elements of a new form he terms his "total art." Similarly, many contemporary international artists are actively refusing to have their work defined as either design or art—categories they feel are misleading and far too restrictive. As we move forward through the twenty-first century, distinctions between design and art are likely to become increasingly difficult to define.

1. As the topic is such a vast one, the discussion in this book is limited to the work of significant visual artists who have worked, since the late 1960s, in the idiom of minimal, austere, geometric abstraction.

2. Kubler 1962, p. 1. Among the thousands of books in Donald Judd's main library in Marfa, TX, are various works on George Kubler and his essential writings.

3. *Ibid*. pp. 1–2.

4. Arthur C. Danto, quoted in Peter Joseph, Foreword, A/D Gallery catalogue, September 1992, pp. 4–5. Danto also notes that, of the three forms listed by Giorgio Vasari in *The Lives of the Most Excellent Painters, Sculptors and Architects* (1550), architecture was considered the highest art form.

5. See Wilton-Ely 1993.

6. Danto, *op. cit.* note 4, pp. 4–5.

7. For further discussion of the role of the decorative arts and design during this period, see Silverman 1983.

8. Quoted in Benjamin 1987.

9. See Troy 1991.

10. See Rose 1965.

11. Duchamp 1973, p. 141.

12. Krauss 1977, pp. 78 and 80.

13. The version Judd owned and hung in his home was a 1964 edition by Arturo Schwartz.

14. See Poling 1983. Kandinsky maintained a more decorative approach to his applied designs than did his contemporaries Kasimir Malevich, Nikolai Suetin, and Ilya Chashnik, who also worked on porcelain design. Their works functioned more as a totality than Kandinsky's porcelains, with their geometric forms echoed in the applied decoration.

15. The work of the Russian avant garde was not well known in the United States until 1962, when Camilla Gray published the first English-language book on the art of the Russian Suprematists and Constructivists, *The Great Experiment: Russian Art 1863–1922*. Judd's library in Marfa, TX, contains a copy of this seminal book. While an art critic, Donald Judd wrote several of the first essays on the work of Malevich and his contemporaries. His library also contains a shelf of books on Soviet architecture.

16. Joost Baljeu, *Theo van Doesburg*, New York: MacMillan Publishing, 1974.

17. Ludwig Mies van der Rohe, quoted in *Time* magazine, February 18, 1951; also at www.creativequotations.com/one/997.htm, active April 2004.

18. A singular element of the organization of the current exhibition has been its coordination with an exhibition of the furniture and decorative work of Josef and Anni Albers, on view simultaneously on the first floor of the museum.

19. Thomas McEvilley, "Yves Klein and the Double-Edged Sublime," Rothko, Klein, and Turrell 2001, p. 77.

20. Donald Judd, "In the Galleries," *Arts Magazine*, January 1963, p. 69.

21. Conversation with Ellsworth Kelly, October 3, 2003. For further discussion of twentieth-century artists who made furniture, see Domergue 1984 and Perreault 1981.

22. Donald Judd, "In the Galleries," *Arts Magazine*, April 1962, p. 87.

23. Discussion by Claes Oldenburg of *Bedroom Ensemble* quoted at http://cybermuse.gallery.ca/ cybermuse/search/artwork_e.jsp?mkey=996, active March 23, 2004.

24. Charlotte Willard, "The Shape of Things to Come," *New York Post*, May 8, 1966.

25. Robert Coates, "The Art Galleries," *The New Yorker*, May 21, 1966.

26. Clement Greenberg, "The Recentness of Sculpture," reprinted in Battcock 1968.

27. The term was first coined in 1927 by David Burliuk, a painter, who defined "minimalism" as the "reducing of painting to the minimum ingredients for the sake of discovering the ultimate, logical destination of painting in the process of abstraction." Graham 1971, pp. 115–16.

28. Sol LeWitt, "Paragraphs on Conceptual Art," 1967, quoted in Legg 1978, pp. 166–67. Meanwhile, in 1966, British philosopher Richard Wollheim's essay "Minimal Art" (*Arts Magazine*, January 1965) characterized the new art of the 1960s as having "minimal art content," but did not differentiate between what we think of today as Minimalist works and Pop art. Terminology was often a contentious point among the artists, particularly those who, like Robert Morris, maintained that his work was "sculpture." Others, who were interested in having their work represent a conscious shift from traditional forms of art, followed Judd's lead and classified their work as neither painting nor sculpture.

29. Judd, quoted in "New Nihilism or New Art?," interview by Bruce Glaser with Donald Judd, Dan Flavin, and Frank Stella, New York, February 15, 1964, broadcast on WBAI New York, March 24, 1964. Los Angeles: Pacifica Radio Archive, Tape #BB3394.

30. Kubler 1962, p. 129.

THESIS: A CHAIR EXISTS AS A CHAIR ITSELF

Because of the influence of his critical writing as well as his work, Donald Judd (1928–94) is arguably the first artist one thinks of when considering the term "Minimalism." In a 1965 article entitled "Specific Objects," Judd, writing as a critic for *Arts Magazine*, threw down the gauntlet, challenging all past art as being "tired/old and done." Although acknowledging that his new work and that of a few contemporaries did not constitute a particular style, Judd declared that it was "neither painting nor sculpture," terming it instead "specific objects." Judd noted that these ascetic, geometrically abstract works shared a new sense of space and materials, and offered the viewer a new and more active role than traditional art.

The primary challenge for many of the so-called "Minimalist" artists was to allow viewers to experience the objects as "real"— so that their physical characteristics conveyed their content and meaning. Judd wanted those encountering his work to have an essentially phenomenological, retinal experience. The austerity of materials and simple, mass-manufactured forms of his "specific objects" were necessary, according to Judd's thinking, to make viewers conscious of why and how one sees. As artist Richard Serra noted, "Judd's work is to be looked at, first and foremost. The experience is always rooted in perception."[1] As a result, a more accurate term to describe this work might be "maximalist," in the sense that the artists were using the minimum of materials and expression in order to maximize viewers' awareness of the vast "amount of pure, physical, mathematical information communicated by the work."[2] (Fig. 22)

Today, Judd's artwork is canonized in museums as representing the apogee of "Minimalist" art. It is little known, however, that, from 1970 until his death in 1994, Judd also designed a large collection of functional objects and furniture. Throughout his career, he often publicly differentiated between his "specific objects" and his furniture, continuing the paradigm promoted by philosopher Immanuel Kant in his *Critique of Aesthetic Judgment* (1790). Kant called for a clear distinction between the fine and the decorative arts, stating, "The chief point is a certain use of the artistic object . . . to which the condition, the aesthetic ideas, are limited, versus painting and sculpture whose main purpose is the expression of artistic ideas . . . and to be looked at."[3]

Judd's frequent, verbal differentiation between art and furniture was influenced by the tenor of the times during which he began designing furniture. In the late 1960s and early 1970s, such prominent critics as Clement Greenberg denigrated new Minimalist work by describing it as "closer to furniture than art."[4] Judd, who was attempting to introduce a new definition of contemporary art, must have interpreted this disparaging comparison with design as a signal that it was not an auspicious time to acknowledge his initial forays into furniture design.

Instead, in an essay entitled "It's Hard to Find a Good Lamp," Judd challenged Greenberg's statement by forcefully stating his thesis that art and design are differentiated through the *intentions* of the creator:

> In the middle sixties someone asked me to design a coffee table.[5] I thought that a[n art] work of mine which was essentially a rectangular volume with the upper surface recessed could be altered. This debased the work and produced a bad table which I later threw away. The configuration and the scale of art cannot be transposed into furniture and architecture. The intent of art is different from that of the latter, which must be functional. If a chair . . . is not functional, if it appears to be only art, it is ridiculous. The art of a chair is not its resemblance to art, but is partly its reasonableness, usefulness, and scale as a chair. . . . A work of art exists as itself; a chair exists as a chair itself. . . . Due to the inability of art to become furniture, I didn't try again for several years. However I've . . . continued to sketch ideas.[6]

In his writing and public speaking, Judd often reiterated Kant's view that art differed in its function from furniture, in that it was "something you look at."[7] His continuing desire to design and manufacture furniture, however, somewhat mitigates such polarizing statements, and offers an interesting contradiction. At various times, Judd acknowledged the parallels between his art and design, affirming, "Of course if a person is at once making art and building furniture and architecture there will be similarities. The various interests in form will be consistent. If you like simple forms in art you will not make complicated ones in architecture [design]."[8] This seeming opposition, between what Judd said and the fact that he continued to design furniture throughout his life, is one of the most fascinating aspects of the relation between his works of art and design.

22. Donald Judd, *Frame Table and Chairs, in situ* in private home, New York

23. Donald Judd, *Wintergarden Bench #16/17*, 1984. Douglas fir

23

Judd made a substantial volume of artwork for fifteen years before taking on furniture design. As in the case of a number of artists featured in this book, the furniture evolved out of his need for functional objects as he acquired buildings and transformed them for his own use. For Judd, his furniture was primarily a branch of architecture, as both were intentionally functional and engaged the surrounding space.

In initiating both his design and his artworks, Judd made quick sketches on paper, creating an abbreviated vocabulary of basic forms, without any implied references or emotion. For both kinds of work, Judd insisted that the materials he used and their surfaces be read as "themselves," and not act as illusions of some other material or somehow convey metaphoric meanings.[9] As he said in reference to Dutch artist Piet Mondrian, Judd wished to eliminate all dichotomies and referential categories in all of his work: "A shape, a volume, a color, a surface, is something itself. It shouldn't be concealed as part of a fairly different whole."[10] (Fig. 23) While eschewing narrative, the basic subject matter of Judd's work was its emphasis on perceptions of space, volume, light, color,

and materials. In his serial pieces, the content was largely based on variations on a single theme.

In the early to mid-1950s, following his graduate training in art history and philosophy,[11] Judd focused on exploring the nature of art and discovering new forms of making it. Judd initially painted on canvas, featuring swatches of colored, curved, and straight lines. He later described these as "half-baked abstractions."[12] Gradually, over the next few years, the artist abandoned his early series of paintings in Liquitex, oil, and sand (fig. 24), as he grew to feel that they did not properly "occupy space."[13] Instead, he began making his "specific objects": freestanding works of art that he considered a new art form. These early works were made in wood, painted cadmium red, and they often included found metal discs, pipes, and pieces of iron (fig. 25). In 1963, Judd's first solo exhibition of his "specific objects" at the Green Gallery in New York received critical acclaim. By 1964, Judd was using galvanized steel and iron, often painted with red enamel or sided with colored Plexiglas, in his pieces. All were fabricated in a metal shop according to the artist's specifications. Works from this period also include pristine, hollow, thin sheet-metal boxes and stacks (fig. 26).

Wanting an area big enough to show his increasingly large-scale work, Judd bought a cast-iron building on Spring Street in Manhattan in 1968. The artist stripped the structure down to its core and added new wooden floors on several of its five stories. Within the loft space, Judd used walls to portion off small bedrooms for himself and his two children, Rainer and Flavin. He placed a ceramic-footed bathtub and a toilet in separate rooms across the hall from two small sink/closet spaces. In 1971, Judd designed a pair of identical, stainless-steel shelf-and-sink combinations for the latter (fig. 27). As he noted, "These were designed directly as sinks. . . . I didn't confuse them with art. The base of the sink is an ellipse, which so far I've never used in art, instead of a circle, which I do use."[14] Judd also made some very simple furniture, including several versions of a Cor-ten steel chair, which he ultimately rejected.[15]

The early stainless-steel coffee table, which Judd describes in his famous statement (cited above) as having been a failure, had a complicated genesis. Around 1970, Warhol celebrity Jane Holzer asked several artists to make functional design work. Judd took one of his existing brown, steel artworks, designed

24. Donald Judd, *Untitled (DSS 26)*, 1961. Cadmium red Liquitex and sand on plywood

25. Donald Judd, *Untitled*, 1963. Oil and plywood with iron pipe

26. Donald Judd, *To Susan Buckwalter, 15 December 1965 (DSS 56)*, 1970. Blue lacquer on aluminum and galvanized iron

27. Donald Judd, *Spring Street Sink and Shelf*, 1970–71. Stainless steel

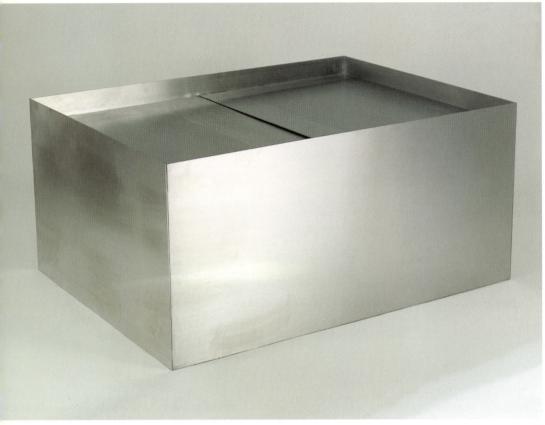

28   29

with a 2½-inch (6.4-cm) recession along its top edge, and remade it into a coffee table (fig. 28). To increase functionality, he split the top into two parts that slid over one another, thereby providing storage space. As none of his artwork had moving components, for Judd, this distinguished the work as functional. However, as he has stated in numerous essays, he then decided that it was an unsuccessful table, and "destroyed" it. Nevertheless, his regular repetition of this story indicates that the table-making and its relationship to his works of art continued to hold significance for him. In addition—just as he would revisit earlier forms in his later works of art—Judd returned years later to the basic form of this coffee table in several pieces of furniture. In 1985, for example, for his Spring Street home, Judd adapted the initial coffee table's recessed top for a wooden serving cart, and designed a serving table in which the top slides open to reveal storage space for plates and glasses within (fig. 29).

In 1974, Judd bought his first building in the small Texas town of Marfa, where he also purchased thousands of acres of land, a number of downtown buildings as studios and living quarters, and two outlying ranches. Once there, he began

28. Donald Judd, *Untitled (Double Coffee Table)*, 1970–71. Stainless steel

29. Donald Judd, *Wooden Serving Table/Cart*, 1985

30. Donald Judd, desk by Judd with Rietveld chair, *in situ* at Marfa, TX

30

experimenting with architecture, noting, "I have a lot of my own work and I want it installed properly. Then I have quite a bit of other people's work, and it takes a lot of space. I'm very serious about this, and that's the main reason why I keep getting more space."[16]

Judd later claimed that the initiation of his furniture design was prompted by the fact that in Marfa and its surrounding areas, "There was no furniture and none to be bought, either old . . . or new, since the few stores sold only fake antiques or tubular kitchen furniture with plastic surfaces printed with inane geometric patterns or flowers."[17] However, most of the rooms in Judd's homes and studios in both Spring Street and Marfa include many functional objects, particularly chairs, by significant designers he admired and collected, such as Gustav Stickley, Gerrit Rietveld, Marcel Breuer, Ludwig Mies van der Rohe, Rudolph Schindler, and Alvar Aalto (fig. 30). In some cases, Judd was among the early American collectors of these European designers' works.[18] Further contradicting his statement that he did not have access to fine furniture in Marfa, Judd regularly had trucks transport supplies and belongings between New York and Marfa, and thus could easily have

furnished his Texas homes with items he purchased in New York. He filled his buildings in Marfa and the two Texas ranches with his own designs and those of designers he admired, and numerous inexpensive chairs that he was able to purchase easily in Mexico, just 15 miles (24 km) away.[19] He continued to design functional work because the challenges and aesthetics interested him, rather than because of any shortness of supply.

One of Judd's first furniture designs in Marfa was a double-sided, wooden platform bed for his two children, with a wall dividing it into two private compartments (fig. 31). The following year, the artist designed and hammered together small desks for the children's rooms in the Block complex, a walled compound containing various residential areas and a studio, library, and gallery (fig. 33). Judd built the desks as simply as possible, with their design inspired directly by the inherent qualities of the available materials. The desks' structure was determined by the proportions of the wooden planks he purchased from a

31. Donald Judd, *Children's Double Platform Bed*, 1977. Pine

32. Donald Judd, prototype for *Child's Desk*, detail showing nails

33. Donald Judd, prototype for *Child's Desk*, 1977. Pine

lumberyard, and he assembled the finished work without changing the wood in any way other than making a few small cuts (fig. 32).[20] These few works are among the only pieces of furniture that the artist made himself, and many of their forms echo those of his earlier "specific objects."

The children's desk remained the basic form of all of Judd's subsequent desk designs. Their shelf structure, with a second level directly under the top, conveys a sense that the top is "floating." Judd had earlier experimented with this concept in his artwork, when he designed a series of simple, geometric plywood box forms in 1976 (fig. 35). Each was made with slight variations: some open at the top, others with an overhanging top and bottom, and several with the top slightly raised, so that it appears to float above the plywood sides. The use of this open, layered, recessed space was often explored by Judd in various works of art, desks, and tables throughout the next two decades (fig. 34).

Judd used the architectural spaces in the buildings he renovated as a means of establishing what he felt were the appropriate ways for displaying and living with his art and furniture designs. Each room became a setting in which to install his work and/or furniture "properly"; and each installation was closely tied to his sense of proportion within the space (fig. 36). Many of his domestic areas in Marfa are intimate and occupy quite small rooms, the opposite of the areas in which he installed his works of art. Nonetheless, each room is clearly arranged as an installation, where the architecture is a key element in experiencing the objects inside. In general, in the domestic areas Judd placed his own furniture, and that of the designers he admired, in a manner inviting such activities as dining in large groups, reading and sleeping near woodstoves, talking to visitors while working in the kitchen, and so on. As Roberta Smith recently noted, "Judd wanted to create a world that was entirely self-sufficient, and he achieved this in Marfa."[21]

In New York and Texas, Judd reconsidered the design of everything within the spaces, designing not only the art, but also a great deal of the furniture, porcelain cups, saucers, plates, and even refillable glass bottles (figs. 37, 39).[22] Wanting nothing to be hidden or unavailable to the viewer's gaze, Judd remained committed to having all his creative resources, as well as the "whole" ensemble, readily visible. Therefore, with few exceptions, Judd designed his objects, tables, and desks, in both metal and wood, with open shelves instead of drawers. As in

34

35

34. Donald Judd, *Steel Box*, Marfa, TX, one of a series produced between 1972 and 1982

35. Donald Judd, *Plywood Box*, 1974

36. Office of Clarence Judd Architects, Marfa, TX

the case of his works of art, the visible interiors of Judd's furniture invite viewers to "experience" the work by moving around it, and seeing it from all four sides.

During the 1980s, as Judd bought and restored additional buildings in Marfa, he continued designing furniture that he and his family used, but which he did not fabricate himself (see *Chair #48*, p. 168). Beginning in 1982, Judd designed a number of chairs, benches, beds, and tables in sheet metal and copper, later stating, "This was for myself but also was the first furniture to begin as furniture to sell."[23] The furniture was made in limited editions, and Judd never allowed it to be exhibited in art galleries alongside his works of art; consequently, it was never publicized or given the visibility of the latter. This can be explained, in part, by the fact that although the role of the "artist as celebrity" evolved during the 1970s and 1980s, it was not a time for the ascendance of design.[24] As a young, ambitious artist, Judd would probably not have wanted to diminish the reception of his art with any potential confusion with his furniture. In addition, Judd may have been concerned that people would purchase his design work and treat it as artwork—only less expensive—which went directly against his thesis that design was to be functional, while art was not. As Judd later noted:

> I am often asked if the furniture is art, since almost ten years ago some artists made art that was also furniture. The furniture is furniture and is only art in that architecture, ceramics, textiles, and many things are art. We try to keep the furniture out of art galleries to avoid this confusion, which is far from my thinking. And also to avoid the consequent inflation of the piece.[25]

Judd conceded, however, that "the forms of art and of non-art have always been connected . . . the separation is due to collecting and connoisseurship."[26]

In the 1980s, Judd became acquainted with the Lehni Company, near Zurich, Switzerland, which made very high-quality, simple metal furniture. Judd was intrigued by the company's precision metal-bending technology. Deciding that this process would be useful in designing and making his furniture, he had them fabricate a number of new works (fig. 40). This precise bending of the metal also served as the inspiration for Judd's wall-hanging *Swiss Pieces*.

Judd continued designing furniture throughout his life, varying the quality of the materials, colors, and price (fig. 41). In general, the furniture Judd made for

37. Donald Judd, porcelain plates, 1990

38. Interior view of Donald Judd's Spring Street studio, New York, fourth floor

39. Donald Judd, porcelain cups and saucers, 1990

40. Installation view, Marfa, TX, showing Lehni colored boxes in studio

41. Donald Judd, installation view, A/D Gallery, New York

his own use, particularly in Texas, was of pine or plywood, while the furniture for Spring Street tended to be made in stronger, higher-quality woods, such as Douglas fir and mahogany (fig. 38). Gradually, Judd allowed his furniture to be exhibited in a few, select European museums. In spite of the visible contradiction in his work, he continually maintained that "the difference between art and architecture is fundamental. Furniture and architecture can only be approached as such. Art cannot be imposed on them." However, he did occasionally provide clues to his continuing interest and work in design:

> The mistake I made with the [1970 coffee] table was to try to make something as unusual as I thought a work of art to be. Back of this was the assumption that a good chair was only a good chair, that the chair could only be improved or changed slightly and that nothing new could be done without a great, strange effort. But the furniture slowly became new as I dealt easily with the

42   43

reality. . . . I can now make a chair or a building that is mine without trying to derive forms from my own works.[27] (Fig. 42)

In the end, Judd's furniture and design objects, although distinct in intention, appear very similar to his works of art in both form and materials. Given their remarkable range and breadth, it is evident that the artist took his design work seriously. Indeed, as he acknowledged in the 1980s, "I've spent quite a bit of time on the furniture, so I don't consider it frivolous." However, he continued, "I am an artist, and therefore the art is more important. I make a big distinction between the art and the furniture and architecture. I'm careful about taking ideas from art and placing them in another context."[28] By differentiating verbally between art and design, while at the same time keeping his functional designs concealed from the public, Judd was able to continue making both, using a shared language of form and materials (fig. 43).

During the late 1960s, in advancing an extreme view of what separates design from art, Judd laid down a thesis that Scott Burton would quickly counter. This dialogue continues today as an active conversation among many younger artists. Through his persuasive, articulate critical writing and the quantity and austere beauty of his work, Judd still exercises a significant impact on others' work and thinking well after his death. As his furniture and design work gains wider exposure, this will undoubtedly continue.

42. Donald Judd, *Bed #87*, 1991. Wood

43. Donald Judd, interior view, Bank building, Marfa, TX

44. Donald Judd-designed pool at Marfa, TX

ANTITHESIS: FURNITURE=SCULPTURE

Around 1970, several years before Donald Judd's initial forays into design, Scott Burton began working with furniture in the context of performance art.[1] From the beginning, Burton's approach to the relationship of design and art was antithetical to Judd's formal separation of the two. For Burton, all of his "furniture/sculpture" was at once art and design, and equally so; and each work was animated through the coexistence of function and aesthetics. Roberta Smith, one of the earliest and most articulate writers on Burton, described his work as willfully balanced between art and furniture, resulting in "a highly formalized usable object that bristles with aesthetic tension."[2]

Burton's furniture/sculpture can be divided roughly into three "types," which overlap chronologically. The first was his Duchampian use of found objects that he then altered slightly. The second type occupied the middle period of his career, as he both altered organic objects, such as granite boulders, and designed idiosyncratic, geometric furniture. The third was his anthropomorphic furniture/sculpture, with its frank, sexual connotations.

Like Robert Rauschenberg, Burton was initially drawn to art from theatre. His first public recognition came with his *Behavior Tableau*, which featured a group of performers moving slowly among pieces of found furniture. In 1970, in a work titled *Furniture Landscape* (fig. 46), Burton placed existing chairs, tables, and other furniture in a forest setting. Although initially disorienting, the juxtaposition of wood furniture with living vegetation and trees conceptually reinforced the recognition of nature as the source for the furniture's original construction.

In 1972, Burton cast in bronze a "found" Queen Anne-style chair, which he salvaged from a former apartment tenant, and set it outside the Artists' Space gallery in Manhattan. Primarily conceptual in nature, the work was replete with contradictions, and challenged the generally held belief in the boundaries between the useful and the useless object. Although set like street refuse on the sidewalk, the eighteenth-century-style "chair" was too heavy for passers-by to carry away — thus impractical as a functional object. Nor was it particularly comfortable.

The following year, Burton decided to begin designing furniture himself, rather than using existing objects. Like many of his contemporaries, Burton was not interested in carving or assembling his work, but had it fabricated by others, thereby minimizing the mediation between himself and the finished piece. Burton was primarily concerned with creating work that implied the context of everyday use and domestic function, but also functioned as art. This decision, he later acknowledged, was "not an easy decision and was misunderstood at first."

Burton's work shared many of the qualities of Minimalism, such as geometric, abstract forms, manufactured materials and processes, and a de-emphasizing of the importance of the character and temperament of the maker. However, the artist quickly differentiated himself from others' work, stating, "All my work is a rebuke to the art world." He wanted to move away "from the hermetic, the hieratic, the self-directed" artwork of his more austere peers.[3] Burton further protested, "Art has become a cult, it is a private language that is learned by art lovers. The important thing is to make art that is intelligible to a non-art audience."[4]

Although he, like Judd, wished to "invent a whole new type of furniture for my place and time in American history," Burton nonetheless wanted above all to bring social meaning and public relevance back into art.[5] Believing that the social and political times were potentially "proceeding towards apocalypse," and that most contemporary art was "spiritually insufficient in a doomsday climate," Burton insisted that new art "have a new, more engaging relationship with its audience," and be "more outer-directed, less self-important." Burton felt that by changing art into a visual culture of design and incorporating audience participation, contemporary art would "take an increasingly relative position. It will place itself not in front of, but around, behind, underneath the audience — in an operational capacity."[6]

With its anthropological nature, resting literally "underneath" the human body, the psychologically charged chair became both a central idiom and an essential theme of Burton's work. As Brenda Richardson noted, Burton was passionate about the possibilities inherent in his "sculpture in love with furniture." As he provocatively stated, "My emotional core is always in the furniture object. I couldn't do a 'sculpture' if you asked me to."[7] At the same time, Burton used his status as an artist to distinguish the power and inventiveness of his work from that of designers and craftsmen, maintaining that they "need to have some

46

45. Scott Burton. *Two Curve Chair*, 1989. Lacquered hot-rolled steel

46. Scott Burton, *Furniture Landscape*, 1973

47. Scott Burton, *Lawn Chairs (A Pair)*, 1976–77

47

common sense, whereas I rarely abandon an idea on the grounds of impracticality. I don't have to think in rational terms: I can do whatever I like."[8]

For his first solo gallery exhibition, consisting of two chairs and two tables, Burton described his work as "pragmatic structures," thereby blurring their categorization as either furniture or art. In 1976–77, the artist made a series of chairs, including *Lawn Chairs (A Pair)* (fig. 47), based on the Adirondack prototype. No one was making Adirondack-style chairs at the time; however, Burton saw their inherent sculptural qualities.

Burton's frequent use of luxurious, sensuous materials and sophisticated forms also distinguishes his work from that of his more Minimalist contemporaries. Each of his furniture/sculptures has a "distinct personality."[9] In 1977–78, he designed a spare, ivory-tiled side table, and *Inlaid Table* (fig. 48). The latter is a tall, rectangular form made of galvanized steel, echoing the strict geometry and materials of Judd's metalwork. In a witty play on materials, Burton's table is inlaid at the bottom edge of each side and on its top surface with precise squares

48

49

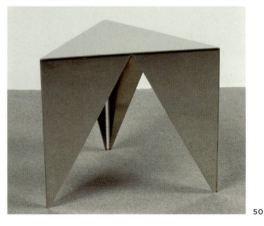

50

of mother-of-pearl. With its *trompe l'œil* niches of opulent material, Burton's table appears as a more elegant rendition of, and wry spoof on, the spatial ambiguity of Richard Artschwager's earlier work, *Pink Tablecloth,* of 1964 (fig. 49). In Burton's hands, the mundane plastic Formica delineating the different parts of Artschwager's solid rectangle is now replaced by sophisticated, opalescent, jeweled forms.

In 1978, Burton designed his geometric *Child's Table and Chair* (fig. 51) in painted and lacquered wood and stainless steel. The idea for children's furniture was based on the artist's memory of a tiny table and chair that were loaned to him as a child and never forgotten. The delicate pastel colors and unexpected detailing of forms differentiate Burton's work immediately from the materials and processes of work by his contemporaries, such as Judd (cf. Judd's children's desks, pp. 44–45). Moreover, Burton added small, shiny accents on the furniture legs and tabletop, and placed unexpected bright colors and intimate details (such as the slight lip extending over the edge of both table front and chair seat) throughout the piece.

By 1978, Burton was also bending single sheets of hot-rolled steel to create beautifully simple, rounded chair forms, the rusted surfaces of which looked both elegant and rough. During the next decade, he experimented with numerous materials, from concrete and aluminum to highly polished, nickel-plated steel, which he used to design his *Hectapod Table* (fig. 50) of 1982, a visual homage to Isamu Noguchi's 1957 aluminum prismatic tables for Alcoa (see p. 25). Burton increasingly used the materials of the construction trade to make his work, including wood, glass, rubber, concrete, steel, and granite. But his use was always counter to the way in which they were incorporated in contemporary architecture. For example, rather than using granite as a thin "skin" for buildings, Burton used it in solid form for his furniture/sculpture.

In the 1980s, Burton began a series of *Rock Chairs* and *Tables* (fig. 52), in which minimal intervention was made to dense granite boulders to make them functional. Solid, heavy, and impervious to the weather, these works heralded Burton's increasing interest in creating artwork that was site-specific and enabled greater interaction within the public arena. Declaring of his new outdoor commissions that "the social questions interest me more than the art ones.

48. Scott Burton, *Inlaid Table ("Mother-of-Pearl Table"),* 1977–78. Galvanized steel with inlaid mother-of-pearl

49. Richard Artschwager, *Pink Tablecloth,* 1964, installation view, *Primary Structures* exhibition, The Jewish Museum, New York

50. Scott Burton, *Hectapod Table,* 1982. Polished nickel-plated steel

51. Scott Burton, *Child's Table and Chair,* 1978. Painted, lacquered wood, polished stainless steel, and leather

I hope people will love to eat their lunch there," Burton was, by the mid-1980s, one of the main proponents of the new "Public Art." Now describing himself as a public sculptor, Burton began designing functional, large-scale sculpture, intended to be integrated into diverse segments of social, mixed-class interaction, from courtyards and public seating to corporate lobbies and state parks. In a 1980 magazine interview, Burton cited a "new architecturality" in art, which shapes and enhances the viewer's experience, and whereby the active use/function by a viewer becomes the very meaning of the work. Sharing with Judd an abiding admiration for Gerrit Rietveld's work, Burton described the Dutch designer's "furniture-approaching-sculpture" as "the major precedent for any contemporary art object seeking to extend itself toward environment and architectural design. . . . Here is a maximally considered object."[10]

Burton's sinuous, elegant, and simple steel desks and chairs of the late 1980s are the last pieces he designed (fig. 53). As the artist became increasingly ill, his dealer Max Protetch would visit him in hospital every night, bringing in a prototype of a chair, the design of which had been fighting Burton for some time. Two men carried various prototypes into his room, and Burton would get out of his bed in order to sit and test their functionality, until one form gave the chair the proper "spring" he intended it to have.

In April 1989, a year before Burton's death, Museum of Modern Art curator Kirk Varnedoe invited the artist to organize the first of a series of small exhibitions at the museum based on artists' choices from the permanent collections. In his installation entitled *Burton on Brancusi*, Burton exhibited several of Brancusi's pedestals by themselves, rather than as functional objects on which to display the sculpture. This was a visual confirmation of Burton's thesis that typologies of design deserve equal consideration to those of art, and demonstrated that the best in each discipline share many affinities. The exhibition garnered much attention and some controversy, indicating that the hierarchy separating art and functional object was still very much in place. Nonetheless, as Burton once told an interviewer, "I feel very lucky that, at this point in history, what I love best has a new, wider significance. . . . 'Scott. Chairs. Eloquently': that is how I would like my epitaph to read."[11]

52

52. Scott Burton, *Low Piece*, 1985. Polished granite

53. Scott Burton, *Semi-circle Table*, 1988. Steel

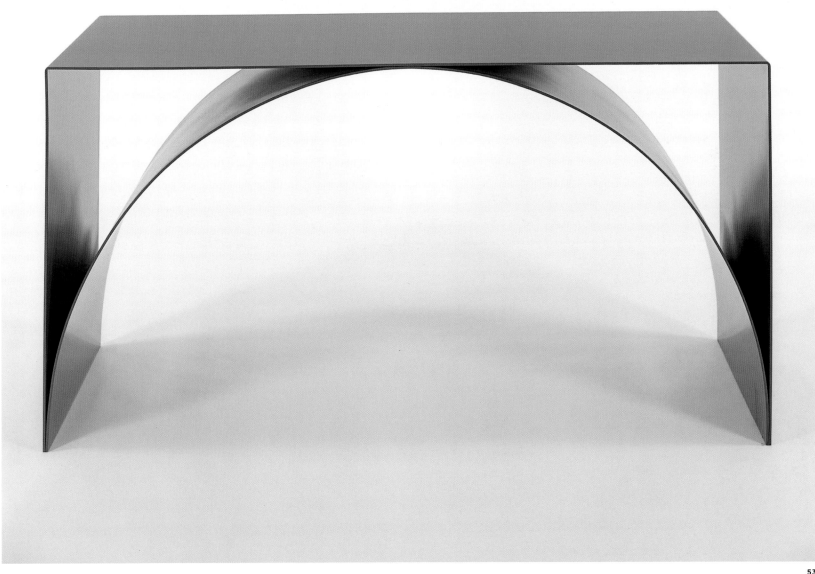

SYNTHESIS: DESIGN AND ART AS "TOTAL ART"

A great designer has to know *everything* (language, history, ethnography, anthropology, psychology, biology, anatomy, etc.), while an artist doesn't have to know *anything*. This polarity . . . is the starting point. But ironically, to really appreciate design, it is *not* about knowledge, but about the experience of living with the work; you don't have to know anything, and you get its 'information' almost though osmosis. Whereas to appreciate a good artwork, you have to bring and apply absolutely everything you know. Why is that?[1]

Richard Tuttle's design work engenders an open-endedness that is appropriate to the concerns of the twenty-first century, and an interest in breaking down the limitations imposed by distinctions and categories. If Donald Judd believed in a clear differentiation between works of art and design, and Scott Burton represented a conscious antithesis of this separation, Tuttle's work exemplifies a synthesizing transformation of these two distinct perspectives into a wholly new form.

Although their restrained execution and materials are often associated with Minimalist tendencies, Richard Tuttle's art and design works are far more intuitive, vulnerable, and personal. Unlike the industrial materials and hard edges of Judd's work, Tuttle tends toward canvas, strange shapes, and easily broken sticks of wood. For him, the Minimalist artists were the end of an historical search that began with Gustave Courbet's intention to break the umbilical cord to art history, and was reaffirmed by Donald Judd. As Tuttle observes, "That was a significant ending and summation; but now we need a new set of ideas, to look beyond the reductive glass and re-explore wider ideas. . . . Minimalism gave us objects, but didn't give us context, such as thinking of space as the frame for art work."[2]

Although he respects the formal purity of the early Minimalists, Tuttle is less interested in their hard-edged, industrial materiality and enormous scale. Instead, his approach is far more insistent on hand-made fragility, modest scale, and an inherent chaos. Tuttle consciously takes Minimalism to the next step: he allows the space and materials that comprise and provide context for the work to trigger emotions, associations, and ideas that arise from within himself, as well as from the viewer. As Susan Heinemann noted, "One doesn't merely 'see' Tuttle's works; one experiences them through one's body."[3]

Tuttle studiously avoids questions about whether his work is painting or sculpture, or how he defines terms such as "fine art" and "design." Rather, he acknowledges that he is interested in "total art," anything and everything in life that has "energy" and "poetic expression." As he observes:

> Indeed, that may be why I do many different things. It is not to be a Renaissance man, but to move forward in the most positive way possible from Modernism's grip without denying Modernism's existence. So "design" (which must be challenged as in the grip of Modernism, as well as the concept of action and reaction moving history) relates to "art" in that they are both part of "total art."[4]

For Tuttle, the most valuable thing is to make something that gives us insight into other people. Therefore, a well-designed lamp is not just referencing design consciousness, but is also directly concerned with that function. As he observes, "Intimate experience of use is why young people today 'get' design."[5]

In 1963–64, Tuttle began cutting and folding pieces of paper into cubes that were small enough to be held in the palm of the hand. This work evolved into plywood reliefs with simple, hollow construction, humble materials, and idiosyncratic contours. By 1967, he was attaching unstretched, often wrinkled, and hand-dyed pieces of material on the walls like drawings (fig. 55). Throughout the 1970s, he also "drew" with wire and string that were stretched across gallery floors, exploring the boundaries between two- and three-dimensional works. Around 1974, Tuttle created the series *Four Summer Wood Pieces* (fig. 56), which Marcia Tucker described as looking "like pieces of furniture hung on the wall,"[6] as they were more volumetric than his other work of the time. However, the forms of these pieces were ambiguous, with no apparent visible function.

In the mid-1980s, Tuttle made a number of freestanding artworks that he called *Floor Drawings* and titled by number. *Six* (fig. 57), created in 1987, is made of sticks of wood formed into a series of triangular peaks, attached by florist wire. Several are covered with rough-stitched, hand-painted pieces of

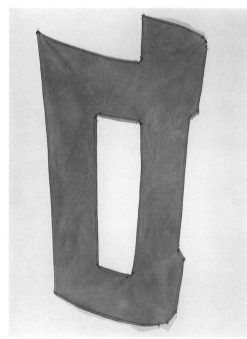

55

54. Richard Tuttle, *Untitled (Chaise Longue)*, 1998–2000, *in situ* in private home, New York

55. Richard Tuttle, *Canvas Dark Blue*, 1967. Dyed and shaped unstretched canvas

56. Richard Tuttle, *4th Wood Slat*, 1974. Plywood and white paint

57. Richard Tuttle, *Six*, 1987. Acrylic paint, florist wire, nails, canvas, corduroy fabric, linen thread, and wood

58. Richard Tuttle, *Floor Drawing #19 (Sentences III)*, 1989. Acrylic paint, wood, ceramic light fixtures, and natural canvas

  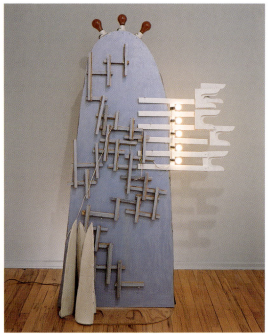

56   57   58

white and black linen. The sculpture, both awkward and appealing, appears as though it could have been made by a child. By terming such work "drawings," the artist signaled that they were artist-made marks that were grounded on, and rise up unambiguously from, the floor. As he said of this work, "The actual physical making of a drawing is very similar to its comprehension."[7]

Tuttle continued his exploration of floor constructions for several years. In 1988, he made a series entitled *There's no reason a good man is hard to find. Number VII* of the series includes a wood stick armature, with several parts that meet at the top and are encircled by wire. The following year, Tuttle began another mixed-media series of constructions that sat on the floor, entitled *Sentences* (fig. 58). He created these from myriad small wooden sticks, Styrofoam, polyurethane, commercial light bulbs, and ceramic fixtures. All are electrified and light up when plugged in, further muddying the separation between art and design, and presaging his later lamps.

While engaged on these series, Tuttle became intrigued with the idea of working with light and its physical properties. For the artist, light is a vehicle for enlightenment, and a symbol of perception and revelation. In discussing his work, Tuttle often references the metaphoric play of sight and blindness with light and insight. While he was organizing an exhibition of the ground construction series, Tuttle began imagining a new lamp structure. Deciding, like Judd, that it is "difficult to find a good lamp," and that "all the ones in the stores are ugly," Tuttle resolved to create his own. The resulting designs all began with the artist's exploring how light bulbs can be used "off the grid," how the bulb exists "as a thing in itself," and how to investigate the light's relationship to its ground.

All of Tuttle's work references ideas of knowledge, introduced by the artist in the elements of the object's construction and in the wider associations the finished work and its materials call to mind. In 1988, Tuttle designed *Mei-Mei's Lamp* (fig. 59), naming it after his wife. In this functional work, he used the same simple wood pieces that he used to construct his contemporaneous artwork. For the artist, *Mei-Mei's Lamp* references the Bauhaus in its look and materials, as well as the history of electricity. The lamp is constructed very simply, with drywall screws, wood, a molded glass shade, and coiled black cable. Tuttle describes it as more of a "piece" than a lamp, "like a fish carrying its own lamp on the bottom of the sea."

Throughout the structure of *Mei-Mei's Lamp*, there are subtle "plays" that are only revealed through extended viewing. The central element holding the lamp, for example, does not touch the ground, but balances on a thin strip of wood, which is attached at either end to horizontal wooden strips. The latter are set a few inches off the ground by short vertical pieces that slalom on opposing sides of the central strut. Tuttle chose the lamp's shade because its glass reflects and throws light in various directions — reminding him of how Cézanne's brushstrokes fractured light—and that "light-fracturing is a kind of relativity common to the era when electricity was replacing gas."[8]

In 1990, the artist made his second lamp, *The Smell of Trees* (see p. 183, fig. 178). As with *Sentences III,* the work is largely vertical, and its construction

59. Richard Tuttle, *Mei-Mei's Lamp*, 1989. Pine, 1890s molded glass shade, sheetrock screws, electrical wire, and plug

61   62

60. Richard Tuttle, *Lamp with No Style*, 1994, *in situ* in private home, New York

61. Richard Tuttle, *Seven-light Chandelier*, one of a series made from 1991 to 1998. Blown milk glass, iron, aluminum disc, electrical cord, and parts

62. Richard Tuttle, *Masculin*, 2000. Maple plywood and plastic laminate

appears rough-hewn, rather than carefully considered. Tuttle cast the edition of twelve lamps in his New Mexico backyard. He acquired some aluminum ingots, then melted and poured them into a mold he had built in the ground. The results are three vertical, saw-toothed, flat columns that remain vertical via the notching of small, thin, seemingly fragile horizontal scrims.

As a further addition to the lamp's design, Tuttle placed this angular construction on to a ceramic plate made by a local potter, with the light bulb initially resting on the platter. He soon discovered, however, that this was "blinding" for the artist, and as he ironically observes, "Artists don't want to be blinded!" Tuttle then experimented with extending the electrical cord up the side of the aluminum, with the bulb dangling down into the interior of the work's vertical center. The result allows him to enjoy "how the light gets caught in all the surface pits made from casting aluminum directly from Styrofoam, and how the light changes the room with its odd fragments here and there. . . . In some way, the light is supposed to return to the original platter like a biological cell having discharged its light for some historical cause . . . expressing the motion of how we feel when we throw on a light switch in the first place, the emotion we feel when we have the smell of trees in our nostrils."[9]

Tuttle's third standing lamp, *Lamp with No Style* (fig. 60), has also gone through various iterations. Made of solid rectangles of wood, the lamp is both heavy and playful. Raised on tiny ball feet, the massive body is made to appear lighter by the large, empty space at its center, and via the three flat boards on the lamp's side that appear to "ruffle" like feathers. Curiously, neither the electrical wires nor the fixture/bulb is neatly hidden within this massive wooden construct, but are placed alone on the opposite side of the wood plank extending out from the top of the entire form. The result suggests that the light is powerful enough to "balance" the weight of the opposing wood structure. In the lamp's latest incarnation, Tuttle has drilled triangular holes through the wood plank above the interior light bulb, letting "out" the light, so that it scatters and reflects off the ceiling above. The act of turning the lamp off and on has a physicality that intrigues Tuttle by "joining the world of ideas and science, and refreshing both."[10]

Following the example of his *Floor Drawings*, Tuttle has also developed a series of chandeliers, characterized by suspended, graphic, forged-iron "drawings" in space (fig. 61). The artist initially constructed a maquette using wood and sections of PCB pipe to emulate blown-glass cylinders. Over the last decade, the character of the chandeliers has fluctuated, as the artist has added differing numbers of hanging glass tubes, extending the graphic syntax of the wrought iron.

In addition to various forms of lighting, Tuttle has designed other functional objects, ranging from the rugs to chairs. Tuttle's wool *"Is there a . . .?"* rug (fig. 64) is based on his long-standing admiration for the way Islamic floor coverings "hold their own space." The artist wanted the design of his carpet to be "in" the weaving, rather than applied on top. He therefore instructed the weavers to spin one strand of chemically dyed yarn along with the undyed yarn in the three-part weft. This created a field of subtle color that abuts another field of naturally dyed indigo, creating a "line" between them. As Tuttle observes, "We live in this world where the artificial is so important, and yet we can't break away from the natural, so I made a rug where the line between is in adjoining colors."[11] At the same time as designing the rug, Tuttle created a body of art that he titled *New York/New Mexico: The Conjunction of Color*. The privileging of color in both his rug and his artwork reinforces the symbiotic relationship between Tuttle's art and designs.

In 1994, Tuttle designed his *Mesa Chair* (see p. 178). Although simple in form, the work has moved through variations in size to arrive finally at a proportion the artist believes is "right, so that the grain of the wood becomes pictorial because of the rightness of size; it's quite magical. When I sat in it I felt I was on the mesa." The rounded, triangular back piece of the chair extends straight to the floor. It is slightly inclined, so that it appears to be held tentatively from falling back by the

63. Richard Tuttle, *The Nature of the Gun*, 1990, installation view, A/D Gallery, New York

similarly rounded curves of the legs. The negative spaces formed by the legs represent the inverted culmination of the back piece, were it closed at the bottom. As Tuttle observes, "Simplicity and complexity are virtually the same thing."[12]

While in Italy preparing for the exhibition *New Mexico Silver/Firenzi Gold*, Tuttle conceived of a suite of benches and a table he titled *The Nature of the Gun* (fig. 63). Inspired by Florentine furniture-making traditions, Tuttle's ensemble references many disparate styles to create what he calls the "final refinement of crate furniture, reflecting the influence of Rietveld and De Stijl." The title comes from the idea that the design of guns is based on a ratio of part sizes, no matter what their ultimate scale. Tuttle's prototype *Gun* suite was initially a standard 3 feet (91 cm) high. Subsequent production pieces have been made in various sizes, but always retain the same proportions. As Tuttle observes, "In my work, proportion and scale are more important than size . . . the only real scale we will ever know is our own scale, the scale of a human being which can be infinitely unique . . . that's why my work is generally directly connected to it."[13] At times, the artist refers to *The Nature of the Gun* as sculpture, claiming that it "holds the room" in the same manner as his works of art. The joints where the planes of wood meet are based on the Asian or Greek key motif. Before its completion, Tuttle wiped white talc into the drying varnish of sections of the wood, creating a delicate, contrasting surface for the seating and table surface. The result is a suite of functional furniture that combines weight with an impression of delicacy.

With the architect Steven Holl, Tuttle is in the midst of designing the Turbulence House, a guesthouse near his home in Abiquiu, New Mexico. At the same time, he is exploring ideas of comfort—how we live in and use our homes, and how far we can push concepts of furniture; in other words, "You don't stay on the surface with furniture, you go *into* the space of a work." In particular, Tuttle is reconceptualizing the politics of a chair, stating, "Some have political neutrality, while another kind of chair is like a servant offering itself to you, or a throne."[14] Tuttle has designed a new piece of furniture he calls the *Turbulence Chair* (fig. 65) for the guesthouse. The prototype consists of two 16-inch (40-cm) hollow wood cubes that are surrounded by soft and hard foam, and then upholstered. When in production, purchasers will choose the upholstery they prefer for the chair, but it

64

64. Richard Tuttle, *"Is there a . . .?"*, 1997. Wool run in cotton warp

65. Richard Tuttle, *Turbulence Chair*, 2003. Fabric, foam, and wood

66. Richard Tuttle, *Textile Couch*, 2002. Poplar, jute webbing, and Italian raw silk on organic cotton cushioning

must contain the dark angular marks that are carefully positioned on the original. The interior of the *Turbulence Chair* is weighted with lead shot so that, as it spills to either side and stabilizes, it audibly "shimmers" like an African rain stick. The chair can be used singly, with three put together to make a sofa, or can be placed on the floor horizontally as a headrest on which to watch television. Tuttle enjoys the *Turbulence Chair*'s combination of comfort and aggression, noting, "If you can figure out how to structure and use it, then its mysteries are revealed."

As in his works of art, Tuttle's furniture and decorative-arts objects always seem to represent a moment of transition, rather than permanence (fig. 66). Tuttle's enjoyment of the challenges inherent in making functional design work is apparent: "I hide my seriousness in my design, and I like that—it is delicious—as the world thinks design is not as important as 'fine art,' but I don't have that problem. Design can be wonderful and very important. My artwork is about *revealing* rather than concealing. But in design I get to *conceal,* which I am very interested in, and don't get to do in my artwork."[15]

The *Masculin* table (fig. 62)[16] visibly demonstrates the synthesizing aspect of Tuttle's work. The blunt, emotionally neutral, rational forms of the piece directly emulate Judd's severe, systemic, rational art and design objects (what Anna Chave referred to as "smack[ing] of certain tropes of masculinism").[17] At the same time, the humorous, asymmetrical form and the mixing of colors and surfaces of *Masculin* recall Burton's furniture/sculpture. Although Judd and Burton's thesis and antithetical views are clearly evident, when juxtaposed they create a new type of form and context in this work. The "adjustable" aspect of the table acts as a joke on these two conflicting aspects, and their relation to the new whole.

Tuttle's art and design work can initially seem so informal, and even modest, that uninitiated viewers may wonder at his extensive international reputation. Neither his art nor his functional designs and furniture draw attention to themselves through the bold lines, muscular materials, and strict geometry that characterize the work of Judd, Flavin, LeWitt, or Artschwager. If one allows time for extended viewing, however, Tuttle's work slowly seduces through its intrinsic eccentricity, thoughtfulness, and affective nature. Tuttle's furniture and design, like his art, are poignant and singularly human expressions of universal consciousness and poetic expression.

DONALD JUDD

1. Richard Serra, *Artforum* 32, Summer 1994, p. 114. Concurrent with the development of the earliest Minimalist works, existentialist philosopher Maurice Merleau-Ponty challenged, "We must return to . . . our immediate experience of the world." (Merleau-Ponty 1962, p. 405.) The importance of such direct interaction with the physical reality—the materials and structure—of a work of art was echoed by Donald Judd, who repeatedly argued that "You can think about it forever in all sorts of versions but it's nothing until it is made visible." Judd, quoted in Battcock 1968, p. 162.

2. Dave Hickey, "The Luminous Body," brochure for the Chinati Foundation, Marfa, TX, p. 154.

3. From the 1952 translation by James Creed Meredith, Oxford, Oxford University Press, pp. 187–88. The author thanks Michael Comforti for this reference.

4. Greenberg 1967, p. 25.

5. According to the Judd Foundation, this was *Untitled (Double Coffee Table)*, made of stainless steel, *c.* 1967–70. Apparently, three versions of this were made, and Judd destroyed one. Peter Ballantine offers another possible explanation of Judd's rejection of this piece, suggesting that its similarities to his works of art might have scared Judd, and so he abandoned it. Conversation with Peter Ballantine in Marfa, TX, November 2003.

6. Quoted in Judd 1993, p. 6.

7. Judd, quoted in Peter Ballantine's unpublished paper, "Judd, Untitled," 1967, p. 1, and a reference to a lecture Judd anticipated giving in Amsterdam in November 1993 when he received the Sikkens Award, given to him by the Dutch paint company.

8. Judd 1993, p. 7.

9. A number of critics following Rosalind Krauss have noted what they describe as contradictions in Judd's statements that art should be anti-illusionary, given the increased complexity of materials and colors in his later work. See Krauss 1966, p. 26. However, with such materials as aluminum and glossy Plexiglass, the reflection is an inherent quality of them, so, for Judd, this was not a contradiction, but merely another example of truth to materials. For further discussion, see Shiff 1999, pp. 8–13 and footnote 40.

10. Judd "Statement," in "Portfolio: 4 Sculptors," *Perspecta*, New Haven, CT, Yale University Press, March/May 1968, reprinted in Judd 1975, p. 196.

11. One of the most thorough discussions of Judd's early education in philosophy and the development of his own intellectual background and beliefs can be found in Raskin 1999 (unpublished Ph.D. dissertation).

12. Around 1958–59, Judd took a piece of found mahogany and supported it with concrete legs to make it functional, thus constituting a very early attempt at designing furniture. Judd's father was a woodworker and, according to Madeleine Hoffmann of the Judd Foundation, he made a small mahogany table, some pine bookshelves, and assorted, simple wood furniture from the late 1950s to 1966, which are listed in the Boymans' catalogue on Judd's furniture as being by Judd himself. (The top of this table, without the concrete legs, is illustrated as #1, Judd 1993, p. 23.)

13. Judd later noted, "In the first place I was tired of that fact that it's a rectangle [*i.e.*, a painting], and in the second that it's so many inches from the wall, and that no matter what you do you have to put something within the shape of the canvas." Unpublished transcript, May 2, 1966, quoted in Roberta Smith, *interview* 6, January 1969, and in Judd 1975, p. 9.

14. There is no information available on why, in particular, Judd chose to design sinks. In a later essay, after prophesying that "everything that manages to survive from the past becomes art," Judd sarcastically observed that "The art of our time, a thousand years from now, will be ceramic sinks and toilets, the only plentiful and durable objects. The ancient masters will be Kohler and American Standard, the latter obviously at the heart of American values." Donald Judd, *Donald Judd, Architecture*, ed. Peter Noever, Ostfildern-Ruit, Hatje Cantz, 2003, p. 25.

15. There remains some question as to the exact date of Judd's earliest furniture design. In a 1984 essay he noted, "Perhaps the first things I made—about fifteen years ago—that were really furniture were some metal chairs and a table." Domergue 1984, p. 101. A drawing for these chairs exists at the Judd Foundation in Marfa, TX. In the 1980s, Judd returned to these forms and had painted-metal versions made in red and blue by a Texas company. In 1969, Peter Ballantine came to Spring Street to work for Judd as a carpenter and subsequently made all of his artwork in wood. The following year, Ballantine made, at Judd's instruction, the artist's bed on the fifth floor, which was one of the first pieces of furniture made for the space, following the laying down of a new wood floor. Consisting of flat boards, one board high and one thick, 3/4 inch (1.9 cm) up from the floor, the walnut bed is nailed to the floor.

16. Domergue 1984, p. 101.

17. Judd 1993, p. 8.

18. Many of Judd's significant collection of chairs and other furniture by a number of designers were purchased as early as the 1960s, indicating that he was among the earliest Americans to acquire major works by twentieth-century designers. Although many of these pieces were purchased from the Barry Friedman Gallery in New York, Judd did buy elsewhere. According to John Weber, on the occasion of Sol LeWitt's 1969 exhibition at the Museum Haus Lange, in Krefeld, Germany, LeWitt was particularly taken with some Rietveld objects on display there. He visited Rietveld in Utrecht, and urged his American artist friends, including Judd, Daniel Buren, and John Weber, to purchase Rietveld works. Judd also had numerous books on the major designers of the nineteenth and twentieth centuries in his library and was very knowledgeable about design history. The author wishes to thank Keith Johnson of *Urban Architecture* for providing this information. In his essay, "It's Hard to Find a Good Lamp," (Judd 1993, p. 9), Judd commented on furniture by major Modernist designers, noting that since the "Mission" style became unfashionable in the 1920s, "there has been no furniture which is pleasurable to look at, fairly available and moderate in price." See also essay in the current volume by Joseph Cunningham.

19. Information provided by Peter Ballantine and Madeleine Hoffmann of the Judd Foundation.

20. The Judd Foundation still refers to Judd's wood furniture of this type as "2 boards," "5 boards," or "7 boards," *etc.*, maintaining Judd's strict adherence to the innate qualities of the found materials.

21. Roberta Smith, "Social, Anti-Social, and Spatial," lecture at the *Minimalism* conference in conjunction with the exhibition at the Museum of Contemporary Art, Los Angeles, J. Paul Getty Museum, May 1, 2003.

22. According to Peter Ballantine, Judd used these bottles to sell Texas "well water" at Dean & Deluca gourmet food stores in New York City. Judd collected numerous books on the Bauhaus artists and other movements that promoted the idea of designing for all aspects of daily life. Although the tea cups were put in limited production (fig. 39), Judd rejected the designs of his porcelain platters (fig. 37).

23. "It's Hard to Find a Good Lamp," Judd 1993, p. 12.

24. The "minimal look" developed concurrently in visual arts and design (particularly fashion innovations by Courrèges and St. Laurent's "Mondrian" designs of the 1960s). In the July 1966 *Harper's Bazaar* (following the April opening of the *Primary Structures* exhibition at The Jewish Museum, New York), articles touted "The New Dazzling Directness" in fashion in which "pure form fashions convey chic with minimal statement for maximal response. All lines clear; all edges clean." The issue included full-page photographs by Francesco Scavullo of male artists posing with spouses or gallery assistants wearing the latest couture fashions. Donald Judd was photographed looking rather tense beside his wife, Julie Finch, who was shown wearing a couture dress with bows along the back. As James Meyer notes, this blending of art and fashion reflected the astonishing speed and ease of commodification of the art world during the 1960s, and the rise of the collector transforming art into big business. It also reflects the accelerated consumer culture of the period, when new techniques of production, distribution, and expanded mass media extended the visual reach of new ideas. The pairing brought the authority of fine art to design, while the glamour and publicity of fashion were now conferred on fine art. Meyer 2001, pp. 19–24.

25. Judd 1993, p. 21.

26. Donald Judd, "Review" of the *Twentieth-Century Engineering* exhibition at the Museum of Modern Art, New York, *Arts Magazine*, October 1964, p. 137.

27. Judd 1993, p. 12.

28. Domergue 1984, p. 101. Editions of Judd's furniture continue to be available through the Judd Foundation. In May 2001, Madeleine Hoffmann of the Judd Foundation created a landmark installation at Andre Balazs's Mercer Hotel in New York by removing the hotel furniture and replacing it with Judd furniture. It was the first time Judd's furniture had been contextualized for public exhibition in a purely domestic setting, with design objects by other artists, such as lamps by Richard Tuttle, James Turrell ceramics, *etc.* Concurrently, A/D Gallery, under Elisabeth Cunnick, organized a similar type of concept exhibition with Judd furniture and work by other artists. In 2003, Andre Balazs invited Hoffmann to create a variation of this installation in the penthouse suite of his new Raleigh Hotel in Miami Beach, FL, during the Art Basel Miami Beach Fair.

SCOTT BURTON

1. According to Max Protetch, Donald Judd would have acknowledged Burton's influence on his decision to make furniture. The author wishes to thank Max Protetch for providing invaluable background and information on Scott Burton's life and work in our numerous discussions over the past year and a half.

2. Roberta Smith, "Scott Burton: Designs on Minimalism," *Art in America*, no. 66, 1978, p. 138.

3. Scott Burton, excerpt, "Situation Esthetics: Impermanent Art and the Seventies' Audience," *Artforum*, January 1980, Nancy Foote, ed., pp. 23–24. There was a clear sense of rivalry between Judd and Burton. Max Protetch terms Burton the "penultimate post-Minimalist," and notes Burton once threw a brick through the window of Judd's Spring Street building. At the same time, Burton traded one of his works with Max Protetch for an early prototype chair by Judd. He would never have traded directly with Judd, but he admired the work. Conversation with Max Protetch, October, 2003.

4. Douglas McGill, "Sculpture Goes Public," *New York Times*, April 27, 1986, p. 45.

5. Domergue, p. 59.

6. Scott Burton, "Situation Esthetics: Impermanent Art and the Seventies' Audience," *Artforum*, January 1980, Nancy Foote, ed., pp. 23–24.

7. Burton interviewed by Robert Campbell and Jeffrey Cruikshank in *Artists and Architects Collaborate: Designing the Wiesner Building*, Cambridge, MA, MIT Press, 1985, pp. 62–66.

8. Domergue, p. 59.

9. Roberta Smith, "Scott Burton: Designs on Minimalism," pp. 138–40.

10. Scott Burton, "Furniture Journal: Rietveld," *Art in America*, November 1980, p. 102.

11. Domergue, p. 59.

RICHARD TUTTLE

1. Conversation with the artist, New York, October 8, 2003. Tuttle is quoting from some remarks made by one of his teachers at the Cooper Union, and adding some of his own.

2. Conversation with the artist, New York, October 20, 2003.

3. Susan Heinemann, "Reviews," *Artforum* 12, June 1974, p. 75.

4. Richard Tuttle, *Twenty Floor Drawings, Richard Tuttle*, exhibition catalogue, Amsterdam, Institute of Contemporary Art, 1991.

5. Quoted from correspondence to the author, January 19, 2004.

6. Tuttle and Tucker 1975, p. 5.

7. Quoted in Tuttle 1987, p. 33.

8. Conversation with the artist, October 20, 2003, New York.

9. The title of the work comes from William Faulkner's *The Sound and the Fury.* In the novel, the narrator Benjy associates "the smell of trees" with memories of his sister Caddy. Correspondence with the author, January 21, 2004, New York.

10. Conversation with the artist, New York, October 8, 2003.

11. Tuttle and Tucker 1975, p. 5.

12. Tuttle, quoted in a review of his "New and Early Work" on Sperone Westwater website.

13. Conversation with the artist, New York, October 8, 2003.

14. *Ibid.*

15. *Ibid.*

16. In 2000, Tuttle made his idiosyncratic *Masculin* table as an edition of ten. The top, which is connected to the lower table by wooden ratchets, is veneered with Formica. Recalling Artschwager's work, Tuttle refers to the higher table as the "art" section, while the bottom, which is constructed of unfinished poplar wood, he terms the design section, as it "functions."

17. Anna Chave, "Minimalism and Power," *Art Bulletin*, March 2000, p. 159.

Many of the other artists designing geometrically abstract functional work since the late 1960s have continued the "dialogue" begun by Judd's thesis that his artwork differed from his designs. Reflecting their idiosyncratic "voices" and personalities, their design objects fall somewhere in the continuum between Judd's and Burton's polarized statements. Some, like Judd, verbally differentiate between their art and design, while occasionally using the same or very similar vocabularies of form, style, and color. Others design functional objects with dual identities, recalling Burton's antithetical response to Judd's work. In addition, reflecting Tuttle's synthesizing of both in a new context and form, a number of artists are creating work that consciously straddles the threshold between art and design, thereby ignoring any defining distinction between the two. By revealing both aspects of their intention, they create a new form, resisting definitions of either. These artists share an interest in the complexities generated by ambiguity of intention, and in the different contexts in which their works of design and art are seen and used.

JOHN CHAMBERLAIN

John Chamberlain laughs when asked what he thinks about Donald Judd's thesis that furniture and art are different because of the need for the former to be functional. He contends:

> Judd just wanted things to be kept pristine, and for people to keep their hands off his work . . . if you believe in the Judd theory, you need to be un-Judded! Everything is functional, or why make it? Although many people say Judd's furniture is uncomfortable, that is its function: to make people sitting in it have good posture. And if you don't believe in art's function, why do you think so many people for centuries came to believe that God was an old man with long, flowing hair except for having seen Michelangelo's artworks?[1]

Chamberlain is known primarily for his massive, imposing metal sculptures made from compressed car bodies, visible in public collections around the world. In 1962, Judd referred to Chamberlain as arguably the best American sculptor under forty.[2] Reviewing an early exhibition, he noted of the main elements of Chamberlain's work, "The folded sheet metal from automobile bodies is

68

voluminous . . . and constitutes an essential form that is less than its bulk requires. It is grandiloquent, proliferating exhaust pipes . . . exceedingly keen on remaining junk, and proud to be confused with an ordinary wreck."[3] Judd admired Chamberlain's use of car parts as primary material and his compression of the metal, revealing its inherent qualities. As he observed of Chamberlain's work, "Nothing is done which will contradict the ordinary appearance of the metal."[4]

In 1979, denouncing museum installations as not being the proper environment in which to present the new minimal forms of art, Donald Judd created the Chinati Foundation in Marfa, Texas, in order to give visitors a pure, in-depth experience of the work of a few artists he admired. To that end, he converted the former barracks and artillery sheds of Fort D.A. Russell into a public foundation, creating a number of separate buildings in which each of a limited number of artists' works could "exist as an example of what the art and its context were meant to be." However, Judd so admired Chamberlain's work that he did

67. John Chamberlain, *Thordis' Barge*, 1980. Urethane foam and cord

68. John Chamberlain, *Parachute Couch*, c. 1970. Urethane foam, canvas, and parachute

69. John Chamberlain at work on urethane foam couches (*Wiley's Islands*), New York, April 16, 1997

not install it with the other artists' installations at Fort Russell, but instead converted a 23,000-square-foot (2100-m²) building in downtown Marfa for its exhibition (fig. 70).

Chamberlain's is the only artist installation in the town of Marfa other than Judd's domestic interiors, and his is the only installation in which a piece of his functional furniture is positioned adjacent to his sculpture. The Chamberlain building includes soaring open spaces for the huge monumental sculptures, two smaller galleries for wall reliefs, and, at its entrance, a large low-ceilinged, horizontal gallery. Inside, a leviathan foam-rubber couch, 40 x 12 x 4 feet high (64.4 x 19.3 x 6.4 m), sits in the middle of the room, with television monitors mounted on either side. The undulating, corpulent forms, covered with white cotton, make the couch irresistibly inviting. By lying back on its molded surfaces,

70. John Chamberlain, Chinati Foundation installation, Marfa, TX

71. John Chamberlain, installation view, Dwan Gallery, Los Angeles, 1966

visitors can watch one of the adjacent televisions, on which a film from 1968 of the artist and his friends runs continuously (fig. 67).

Chamberlain's determination of what to do with different materials evolves from his intuition, as well as the intrinsic properties of the material (fig. 69). "As an artist I am aware that I have to know when to stop, but the deciding factor has more to do with what I present myself with, that is, with the position I get into to deal with new material. . . . An artist makes a spiritual evaluation of the essence within a thing and then he gets it out; that is the outer appearance of the inner essence, and it is the point."[5] The genesis of Chamberlain's foam couch came from his decision in 1966 temporarily to abandon working with metal car parts and begin experimenting with new materials. Over the next seven years, Chamberlain worked with seven different kinds of material, including synthetic polymer resin, aluminum foil, plastic, and urethane foam. As he remembered, "They all looked good, but they never got much attention, as everyone is so enamored with things they already recognize, and [his dealer Leo] Castelli didn't like them, so no one remembers them today."[6] One of the materials Chamberlain explored at length was foam rubber, because of its flexibility: "I quickly realized that I could do something instant with foam—shape it into many things, squeeze it, and poke it so that I could see the outsides, and then tie it in the middle with string, and see if the result comes off well."[7]

Chamberlain made a number of foam sculptures of various sizes (fig. 71). Needing furniture to sit on in his new apartment in New York, Chamberlain took an electric carving knife to a huge foam cube and proceeded to cut its surface into uneven shapes. As he describes it, he then "plopped it down and it [the couch] looked like a small section of the beach, and I could fall over on it like I was eight years old, and I was down . . . the idea was that the couch had to be very large with no hard parts, so that no matter what your size or weight, you could run across the room and jump on to it with no fear of being hurt or of it being too small."[8]

In 1970, Jane Holzer commissioned an edition of Chamberlain's smaller, more manageable couches and had them manufactured in Italy. Instead of being covered with white cloth or parachute material, they were produced in brown suede. As Chamberlain recalls, "I used to do three or four a year by commission for somebody in a particular place. They are great fun to make. . . . Kids and dogs like them a lot." In addition to these foam couches, Chamberlain designed *Table of Contents* and *Table of Tides* (fig. 72). Made of automobile parts with glass tops, these functional tables more closely resemble his characteristic sculpture than the foam couches in their appearance and materials. As he describes his thinking process, "I wanted the sculpture to come up and be on top of the table as well as below it."[9]

In 1996, Chamberlain designed *Tasted Snow* (fig. 73), a twenty-three-piece porcelain place-setting in an edition of one hundred. Each of the pieces is based on a different machine part, with the salad bowl made from a transmission cover and the plates based on the shapes of flywheels. On the surface of the porcelain, Chamberlain picked up detailing in gold and silver, ironically referencing the metal materials of the forms' origins. His similar porcelain sushi service includes a gear-shaped dish for *wasabi* and a pipe-based cup for the green tea.

Noting that he has never consciously differentiated between art and design, but remains very interested in the subject, Chamberlain also feels the discussion is twenty-five years late in taking place. As the artist is quick to remark of his functional work, "We all have a certain vision that shifts over time . . . artists have a completely different way of looking at things. My past work has been concerned with 'getting to the beauty part' by using garbage; perhaps that is why for a long time I've been a 'phantom' artist. I love that people will now get to see this work. . . . Its visibility, particularly in a museum context, is long overdue."[10]

72

72. John Chamberlain, *Table of Tides*, 1993. Painted stainless and chromium-plated steel

73. John Chamberlain, *Tasted Snow*, 1996. Porcelain overlaid with gold, platinum, and copper

"Art is useless; furniture is useful. This statement is a large enough 'basket' to contain the issue . . . useless says it all."[1] At first glance, Richard Artschwager's pronouncement implies that he is solidly in agreement with Judd's segregation of art and design. However, as his work demonstrates, Artschwager is far more interested in the ambiguous, almost arbitrary, names and meanings we give objects, and in how we see and interact with them in different contexts, than he is in creating strict categories. As the artist expresses it, his intention is always to "make art that has no boundaries,"[2] believing it is up to each viewer to interpret his or her relationship to the work.

Arriving in New York in 1949 to practice art, Artschwager decided that he had to find a way to make a living: "One day I passed a lumberyard, walked in, saw great planks of mahogany, and knew what I had to do. Making furniture in a workshop environment would provide a balanced diet of action and reflection, and it was a real job. What I made was, in the most ordinary sense, needed by others, so I had a morally tenable connection to society."[3] In the 1950s, Warren Rubin, founder of the Workbench stores, hired the young artist as a carpenter/designer. Artschwager began building chests of drawers and other furniture in large quantities. A feature of these pieces was the flexibility of the drawers, which had to fit into various configurations of chests and other furniture. Artschwager recalls, "I got good at this. . . . I got the order on a Saturday and by Friday I'd have everything made—it went straight to the person who bought it. This liberated me . . . there were hundreds of them . . . very geometric . . . I made them for about a year."[4] Three of his early commercial furniture pieces—a desk, a set of shelves, and a swivel chair—were included in an exhibition entitled *Furniture by Craftsmen* organized at New York's Museum of Contemporary Crafts in 1957. Three years later, the Catholic Church commissioned Artschwager to make portable altars for ships, which he produced with brass fittings. The artist was excited by the idea that in making these altars, he was designing something that was both functional and ceremonial, going beyond the merely useful.

Eventually deciding to devote himself entirely to his art-making, Artschwager turned away from working with commercial wood furniture and its connotations of craft aesthetics. Instead, he began to explore the possibilities of replicating the illusion of wood surfaces through the use of such synthetic materials as Formica, which he refers to as one of "the great ugly materials, the horror of the age . . . I didn't invent Formica, nor did I make it my own. There was already this huge choice of imagery just waiting. I have written once that wood grain seemed to have passed through and left a ghost . . . I was getting tired of all that beautiful wood; instead, I wanted to create a picture of wood that at the same time was an object."[5]

The underlying "idea" of furniture in its various forms continues to appear throughout his work. As Artschwager noted in the mid-1980s, "A little more than twenty years ago I commenced to make some furniture as art. . . . I wanted to make an image in space that didn't need a privileged place like a painting. It was the kind of credibility I could live with." Artschwager credits his approaching age forty with "a vision— an epiphany —which was to save me from old age, or at least put it off for a while. And the vision was: everything counts. An itchy nose, scratching it; a distant train. A bit of coffee left in the mug. My hand grasping the mug, the thumb providing guidance. Every encounter with another person. It sounds like caring beyond all reason."[6] This realization that "I can't make life longer so I can't throw away time or opportunities"[7] furthered his interest in making things that were useful and useless at the same time; and can therefore be perceived concurrently as furniture and art.

As early as the 1960s, Artschwager was playing with the basic elements of Minimalism and with the perceived distinctions between art and design. In 1962–63, he made *Table and Chair* (fig. 77), in which he mimicked exaggerated wood grain by painting it on the surfaces of found furniture. A year later, he abandoned the concept of using found furniture and instead designed a chair-surrogate sculpture entitled *Chair* (fig. 76). In the work, *faux* wood-grained Formica delineates the back of the chair and its legs, while the seat is indicated by the use of flat, rich, red plastic cladding. This fully mature work was one of a series of similar sculptures based on furniture models. In each case, such as with *Pink Tablecloth,* Artschwager initially designed plywood rectangles that he then covered with variously colored and patterned Formica. The *trompe l'œil* illusion of space between the legs of the chairs and the tables was suggested by flat pieces of black Formica.

In the celebrated *Primary Structures* exhibition in 1966 (fig. 78), Artschwager's work was included along with that of numerous other artists, such as the austere

75

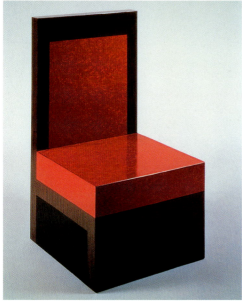

76

74. Richard Artschwager, *Chair/Chair,* 1987–90. Red oak, Formica, cowhide, and painted steel

75. Richard Artschwager, *Desk,* 1950s. Wood

76. Richard Artschwager, *Chair,* 1963. Formica on wood

77. Richard Artschwager, *Table and Chair,* 1962–63. Acrylic on wood

galvanized-iron progressions of Donald Judd, the spare fluorescent tubes of Dan Flavin, and the precise cubic structures of Sol LeWitt. Rather than using natural wood and manufactured or commercially available lights, however, Artschwager photographed the surfaces of real materials (such as wood grain and paint) and transferred them on to a prefabricated, inexpensive plastic laminate. He then used this to cover the exteriors of his sculpture, thereby making his three-dimensional "pictures of furniture" that resemble functional objects but are not inherently functional.[8]

78

Throughout the 1960s and 1970s, Artschwager alternated between creating objects and making "paintings" with acrylic on Celotex. Their subject matter was usually furniture, architecture, and domestic interiors. As with his Formica objects, the challenge for the artist in these paintings was "to bridge the gap between functional and non-functional. That was my interest and that was my radicalism . . . forms were not dictated but were offered up by virtue of where I was in the furniture workshop and by what materials I had available. Very consciously I allowed those things to determine what got done. I was enchanted with the idea of how art arises as opposed to the notion of art as a received body of art history, criticism, and accredited works."[9]

79

In the 1980s, Artschwager returned to designing works that appear to be equal parts furniture and art, with an increasingly unobtrusive use of materials blurring the boundaries between the two. In works such as *Tower III (Confessional),* the artist continued to cover the parts' wooden structure with Formica. However, the laminate's wood grain is far more subtle and realistic than in his earlier work, thus the realization that it is not really wood comes only through close viewing of the work's surfaces. The artist also made a series of works in editions, including, in 1989, several clocks that originated from the idea of a generic mantel clock (fig. 79). But, as the artist describes it, "Where the mantel clock uses its arms to architecturally stabilize time and keep it anchored to the ground, the *Klock* has wings—it's a strange bird caught in flight. . . . It is the essence of time frozen into a stationary object. But you can't freeze time; the *Klock* keeps on ticking."[10]

Ultimately, Artschwager's differentiation between functional and non-functional objects is largely based on how one chooses to use the work, whether

80

78. Installation view, *Primary Structures* exhibition, The Jewish Museum, New York, 1966. Left: Richard Artschwager, *Pink Tablecloth*, 1964; center: Anne Truitt, *Sea Garden*, 1964; right: Paul Frazier, *Pink Split*, 1965

79. Richard Artschwager, *Klock,* 1989. Formica and enameled wood, with clock mechanism

80. Photograph showing folding chair used as prototype for Artschwager's *Chair/Chair*

perceptually or literally. As he notes, every object in the world comes with a "set of instructions," indicating how that object can, and should, be approached. Even within his so-called "useless" definition of art, Artschwager reiterates that it is still an object: "Art is not an idea; it is a *thing*. If it dropped on your foot it would hurt";[11] and it carries with it implicit instructions for its use, in other words, "Put me on the wall." He also differentiates his approach from that of Judd, noting, "Judd was interested in essences—the position of a philosopher. I concern myself with phenomena. Events 'happen.' Art happens. It can't be located in the eye (or the ear?) of the beholder. Or for that matter in/on a canvas. But, yes, a canvas can be a catalyst for an art event. Or an instrument for a 'useful' event. Or both at the same time? That is an interesting question."[12]

In 1987–90, Artschwager designed his *Chair/Chair* (fig. 74) in red oak, Formica, cowhide, and painted steel as a piece of functional furniture. The design is based on a similar folding chair designed in or around the 1920s that was once owned by his family. The prototype that inspired him only exists in photographic form in one of his father's old snapshots (fig. 80). The artist spent about three years working on the chair design, making endless revisions until, as he jokes, "It became a chair story that was told and re-told, and each time the story was told, something got changed." The final version was produced in an edition of one hundred, and, as Artschwager observes, "This is a chair, defined in the moment and configuration; it is a place to put your butt, feet, and back, implied in its form."[13]

In the end, when confronted with both Artschwager's functional chair and one of his furniture-resembling sculptures, it remains difficult to make a full distinction between them. The artist acknowledges this, claiming that his intention is to place the onus on the viewer to decide what is to be viewed and what is to be used, suggesting, "If you sit on it, it's a chair; if you walk around it and look at it, it's a sculpture. . . . You have to look at them either as images or as things. These are initially contradictory, so shut up and *look*; and then, once you have done that, both the image-ness and the object-ness can be co-present without contradictions. In fact, the more layers of meaning, the better."[14]

Having coined the term "conceptual art" to describe his work, Sol LeWitt maintains, "What the work of art looks like isn't too important. It has to look like something if it has physical form. No matter what form it may finally have it must begin with an idea."[1] He continues, "Once the idea of the piece is established in the artist's mind and the final form is decided, the process is carried out blindly."[2] LeWitt's work is often linked to Minimalism due to his focus on objective forms and serial systems; but for LeWitt, the finished work, whether it is considered sculpture, installation, or design, is less important than the initial idea or concept.

Recognized in the early 1960s for his synthesis of conceptual art and Minimalism, LeWitt makes pieces that are more architectonic than anatomical. In the first half of his career, he worked with systems and geometry to emphasize art as object, and to explore every permutation of the cube. In *Objectivity* (1962; fig. 82), LeWitt broke the title word into units of two letters and one of three, and painted them on a dark, red-backed sheet behind a wooden grid, stressing his lack of interest in metaphoric or emotional associations. In *Wall Structure* (fig. 83), he experimented with serialization, which he defines as incorporating multi-part pieces with regulated changes. In this work, he designed constructions of rectangular forms projecting from the canvas. LeWitt limited his early palette to white and black, using mathematical formulae to chart the positioning of cubes within a grid. As his work evolved off the wall and into three dimensions, LeWitt—like other artists in this book—brought to the foreground the relationship of his "structures" with architecture, rather than with sculpture. As he recalled, "I didn't want to think of them as sculpture because they weren't involved in the history of sculpture. My inspirations were in the world of architecture."[3]

LeWitt began experimenting with "dematerializing the object" by having his assistants make wall drawings based on his concept and directions, moving away from the need for the finished work to reflect the artist's gesture and handiwork. As he observed, "The underpinning, theoretically, is to separate the idea of art from the idea of craft. Not that craft is a lower or less exalted activity, but there is a difference. . . . The architect doesn't build the building. The composer doesn't play the instruments."[4] Like Donald Judd, LeWitt was drawn to the idea

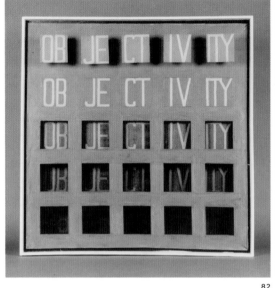

of materials reflecting what they are: "Obviously a drawing of a person is not a real person, but a drawing of a line is a real line."[5]

LeWitt began designing furniture entirely for practical and pragmatic reasons. As he told an interviewer, "My ideas pertain to order and things of that sort. I make things for myself that I need because I feel I can design them better and make them cheaper than I could buy them. . . . The proportions were determined by what I needed. . . . I've made things progressively for my loft. I think one naturally makes one's environment if one stays in a place long enough."[6] In 1965, LeWitt made his first table, painting a white-line grid on its gray, wooden top. Fifteen years later, he made a white wood table, which he deemed "a follow-up" to the earlier table, for a multiples exhibition at Marion Goodman Gallery in New York (fig. 85). Since then, LeWitt has designed a number of tables, with surfaces that are based on geometric grids — patterns that remain central to his work. As he notes, "My tables have grids in them and are very uncomplicated. The grid makes decisions for you; it's a way of evening out space."[7]

In the 1980s, LeWitt augmented the straight, angular designs of his earlier artwork by including additional motifs, such as circles and triangles. After moving to Italy, LeWitt began adding a wide range of primary colors to his work, transforming entire room interiors into swirls of richly banded hues (fig. 86). As the decade progressed, LeWitt incorporated irregular shapes to his visual vocabulary, and began reproducing his wall designs on functional, freestanding room screens. The pattern on one side of the screens is usually in color (fig. 81),

81. Sol LeWitt, installation view, *Tables (1981–1997) & Other Work*, A/D Gallery, New York, 1997

82. Sol LeWitt, *Objectivity*, 1962. Painted wood

83. Sol LeWitt, *Wall Structure*, 1963. Oil on canvas and painted wood

84. Sol LeWitt, *High Table*, 1992. Walnut

85. Sol LeWitt, *Coffee Table*, 1981. Wood painted white and glass

86   87

while the other is occasionally reproduced in black and white (fig. 87); both replicate forms and designs from LeWitt's non-functional works.

Recently, the scale of LeWitt's work has increased, as has its relationship to architecture. Now the designs, grids, colors, and forms of his earlier work are transcribed on work in all media, from immense, dizzying wall drawings to elegant, wooden *étagères* or high tables (fig. 84). His latest designs for tables reflect multiple variations of line, pattern, and color. LeWitt maintains that "art is not utilitarian. When three-dimensional art starts to take on some of the characteristics of architecture, such as forming utilitarian areas, it weakens its function as art." However, his experimentation with the permutations of rational design has also extended to his designing etched crystal glasses (fig. 88), small boxes, earthenware place settings, and assorted posters for everything from his own exhibitions to flyers for wine and the Mostly Mozart festival at New York's Lincoln Center. Ever cryptic, the artist does not comment on how, and if, his intention for, and view of, his works of art and design differ.

86. Sol LeWitt, *Wall Drawing*, 1983

87. Sol LeWitt, *Folding Screen*, 1986. Black and white ink on wood

88. Sol LeWitt, *Untitled: Set of Four Crystal Glasses*, 2002

For Bryan Hunt, furniture is a window into a daily aesthetic that extends equally to his sculpture. Much as Noguchi balanced two opposing styles in his art and design half a century earlier, Hunt sustains his inclination toward the reductive, abstract, and geometric, with an equal emphasis on biomorphic, organic, even baroque forms. The organic aspect of Hunt's work is known largely through his bronze *Waterfall* sculptures. It is also evident in his *Torchère* lamps, with their bulbous, striated cast-iron bodies and blown-glass shades that ripple like water.

Hunt is also drawn to the austere, abstract, and architectural in his artwork and functional designs (fig. 90). He made his first table as a simple surface in his studio in Venice, California, in 1973. Noting that, as an artist, he already had the tools and materials at his disposal, he proceeded to design furniture as he needed it in order to solve the problem of available working space. For Hunt, this remains the most satisfying reason for continuing to make functional objects.

Early in his career, while working on a nearby bridge, Hunt was deeply affected by Frank Lloyd Wright's Fallingwater house in western Pennsylvania. As a result, much of the artist's aesthetic privileges the integration of architecture and interior design. In designing his long wooden dining table (fig. 89), Hunt recalled Fallingwater's construction in which the different levels of the house looked as though they were hanging within the landscape. Similarly, he constructed the armature to hold up the substantial tabletop so that it appears to "float" above its iron legs, which are echoed by thin, linear "shadow" forms. More recently, Hunt's interest in design has extended to a variety of tables (fig. 91), tabletops, standing lamps, candlesticks, and wax candlesticks, reflecting his familiarity with both minimal and organic vocabularies.

89. Bryan Hunt, *Library Table*, 1984. Maple, mahogany or bleached mahogany, and steel

90. Bryan Hunt, *2 oh 3*, 2003. Wood, synthetic fabric, and leafing

91. Bryan Hunt, *Island Table*, 2004

Joel Shapiro's furniture represents the application of ideas developed concurrently while conceiving and making his works of art. Highly influenced by the Minimalism of the late 1950s and early 1960s, Shapiro's art and design works share clarity of language with many of its original tenets. However, his work ultimately rejects purist notions that art's content is shaped only through its materials, production, and the experience of looking. Rather, he extends Minimalist tendencies by adding personal and societal psychology into the mix with Minimalism's forms and materials. Shapiro is very knowledgeable about, and interested in, the history of design. He grew up in a house filled with Herman Miller pieces, "which was considered very radical at the time"; and he and his wife, the artist Ellen Phelan, own works by Alvar Aalto, Donald Judd, and a number of Danish modern designers. In addition, the furnishings in their country house include Scottish Arts and Crafts pieces.

Like the work of his contemporary Richard Tuttle, Shapiro's art and design can initially appear tender, eccentric, awkward, and even childish, evoking connotations of imminent transition, movement, and the essential underlying rhythms of life. Using traditional materials like plaster, wood, and bronze, Shapiro's initial works of art concentrated on such issues as scale, weight, and position. In his early work, the artist explored a dialogue between his objects, the surrounding space, and overall architecture. However, as Roberta Smith comments, "While the Minimalist object matches real space with real space—an exchange particularly apparent in Judd's work—the space Shapiro creates is . . . a space moved through as much by the mind—or the emotions—as by the body."[1] For his first exhibition, at the Paula Cooper Gallery in 1970, Shapiro hung a series of bracketed chipboard shelves at eye level, each holding a different material. The installation used the shelf as a means of both presenting and forcing an intimate reading of the materials. As a result, the structure and the work were equivalent and integral to each other, thereby giving the work both architectural and functional references.

In the early 1970s, the artist's subject matter turned from abstract forms to easily recognizable objects. Rosalind Krauss has described this work as representing "the furniture of our lives, some of it . . . highly charged with emotional overtones."[2] In 1973, Shapiro placed a small bridge made from a block of cast iron

93   94

on the floor in the vast space of the Institute for Art and Urban Resources in New York (fig. 93). In another early work, Shapiro cast a 3-inch (7.6-cm) iron chair, which was exhibited in isolation on a gallery floor (fig. 94). In an interview he recalled:

> I was thinking about a chair; the chair was about oneness and about singularity. It was placed on the floor and it had an absolute change in scale from what you might anticipate. . . . When I put that chair out into a gallery space, I was insisting on an intimate experience in a public situation. . . . Our bodies and our experience become condensed. The chair evokes physical memory. . . . The scale of the piece is its viability in that size, not the size itself. Viability has to do with the fact that it functions as sculpture.[3]

Shapiro later remarked, "If I had made it into a full-sized chair and exhibited it, it would have been meaningless. . . . There was plenty of chair imagery going around. Its potency was possible because it was small." Beyond the scale of these works, what characterized them conceptually was the play they elicited as structures we recognize from our daily lives, and our acknowledgment of their

92. Joel Shapiro, untitled, 1994. Bronze

93. Joel Shapiro, *Bridge*, 1971–73, installation view, *Joel Shapiro* exhibition, The Clocktower, Institute for Art and Urban Resources, New York, 1973

94. Joel Shapiro, *Chair*, 1973–74. Cast iron

95. Joel Shapiro, untitled, 2003–04 (in process). Plaster

95

functional impracticality. On one hand, we project ourselves into these familiar objects; on the other, we are always aware of this "projection" as an impossible psychological fiction. As Shapiro recalls, "I specifically avoided making them large. I was interested in the image as a projection of thought, of mental space. The discourse between memory and the present was amplified by the small scale. This had no utility other than as a mental exercise."[4]

Shapiro's work in furniture began with making a number of "matter-of-fact, very simple, and pragmatic" worktables, sawhorses, and shelves to use in his studio. Woodworking tools were integral to the making of his sculpture, and so were easily available. More important, he was "not entirely satisfied with placing all work on the floor and found the traditional base too exclusive . . . so tabletop shelves seemed like a viable means of setting the work off from the architecture without turning the work into a venerated object, which bases tend to do." Although his miniature castings of tables and chairs were conceived as exploring spatial and sculptural concepts, Shapiro gradually became interested in the idea of casting "something into something—condensing space . . . I began using furniture as a subject in sculpture and then later became interested in making furniture that has a real function in the real world."[5]

In 1996, Shapiro was commissioned to make a functional table. He designed a coffee table with the intention of creating something that was both utilitarian and that functioned within space (fig. 92). Shapiro began by making a prototype in plaster: "I was interested in making negative legs, in making a work in the negative so it looked like I cast around a real coffee table, and then pulled the cast off. In this way the gestation of the work was radically different from normally putting furniture together."[6] The prototype was then cast in bronze, creating a conceptually complex, yet simple, elegant, and functional table.

While he was exploring surfaces and materials, Shapiro made a plaster prototype for *L-shaped Chair*. As he did not feel the result was entirely successful, the plaster remained in his studio for several years. In 2003–04, he revisited the plaster and worked with variations of the prototype until he felt it had achieved a strong resolution (fig. 95). In its new incarnation, Shapiro built up the form by pouring or "flicking" plaster on the wood construct. The top plaster surface,

96

97

98

96. Joel Shapiro, untitled, 2003–04. Plywood

97. Joel Shapiro, untitled, 2003–04. Walnut

98. Joel Shapiro, *Giraffe 2003.* Wood and metal

which remains flat, has the imprint of wood grain, while the plaster on the underlying surface is applied unevenly, reflecting the fluidity of the material.

During the same period, the artist also designed several, small L-shaped side tables in wood that originated as "cut-offs" from other works: "They are all tables and add complicated issues of anatomy."[7] Viewed on their own, Shapiro found that they were "interesting and not predictable," and so had them made by his assistant Ichiro Kato (who worked with Jim Cooper on early Judd furniture), and finished in cherry (figs. 96, 97). The tables are designed with a radical cantilever, and so placing objects on their surfaces necessitates care, a fact that intrigues the artist. Meanwhile, he has avoided designing any chairs, as "chairs are tough and deal with complicated anatomy — a generic chair just does not interest me."[8]

A public art project in 2003 for New York's Central Park generated a further opportunity for Shapiro to play with furniture design. Along with several other artists and designers, Shapiro was given a simple metal-and-wood park bench and asked to transform it. The results were unexpected; as Shapiro notes, "I don't think a wood bench is the same for artists and designers — artists are more interested in the concept of what a bench is than what it looks like or its function, which is what concerns designers." Rather than just applying decoration, Shapiro completely disassembled the bench. The various parts sat scattered around his studio for three months: "I couldn't apply anything to it and have it be meaningful, so I took it apart and reconfigured its components into something non-anatomical."[9] The result is a construction that climbs 10 feet (3 m) vertically in space, but the parts of which, though readily identifiable, no longer function except as sculpture (fig. 98).

For Shapiro, in order for work to be considered as furniture, it has to have a specific utilitarian aim: it has to function. Ultimately, however, he also believes that the most significant design can transcend its utilitarian purpose and, like the best art, prevail over any limiting definitions by exposing another dimension of our humanity: "I am interested in any object that amplifies human possibility and transcends its form, regardless of whether it is furniture or art. . . . This does not happen with very much art, design, or architecture."[10]

Robert Wilson further confounds the dialogue between art and design by making furniture, specifically chairs, as the central element of his theater sets (fig. 102). As he asserts, "I always had a fondness for furniture, and chairs have been the central image or sculptural element in my work. Sometimes people sit on them; sometimes they're just objects. . . . They can also function on their own as valid, independent works of art."[1] Like Burton's, Wilson's chairs maintain a dual identity as both functional objects and aspect of his theatrical "art." They are often the most prominent objects in his stage sets, and appear to have an authority equal to that of the actors. In general, the chairs' forms develop as portraits of specific characters in the plays, and so have visible, differentiated "personalities." As Wilson observes, "In fact, sometimes you don't even see the actor, you see only the chair."[2] Wilson designed his first chair in 1969 for the play *The Life and Times of Sigmund Freud.* Made of wire and mesh, the chair projected its shadow against the stage wall as it was lowered from the ceiling. Although the same effect could have been accomplished by using a cardboard maquette, Wilson insisted that it be produced as a fully functional chair. In his productions, Wilson consistently obscures the line between an object's usefulness and its artistry (fig. 100). None of the numerous chairs he designs for the stage is merely a prop. Instead, they are always made of substantial materials, ranging from lead to marble. Wilson does not allow for any compromise in terms of the pieces' weight, expense, or difficulty of construction. Beyond their lives as theatrical characters, many of the chairs are produced as limited editions of two to fifteen (fig. 101).

Wilson's *Dining Suite* (fig. 99) was designed as a flexible table that could accommodate small or large numbers of people for dinner. The basic galvanized-steel table has three heights. The side chairs are made from plumbing pipe with plywood seats; on one side, the chairs are supported by brushed-aluminum sheets, with a three-dimensional golden cat's paw. Wilson has also continued a long-term project, *Angel Glassware,* a series of winged drinking glasses, each unique. In his studio, Wilson commingles design objects he admires—some made by anonymous craftsmen, others by some of the most significant designers of our time—with his own chair designs. For Wilson, design, whether of a chair, textile, light, theatrical scheme, or building, is all part of one concern. As critic James Levertt says, Wilson "never says what a thing is, but always asks, 'what is it?'"[3]

100

101

99. Robert Wilson, *Dining Suite*, *in situ* in the home of Paul F. Walter, New York

100. Robert Wilson, *Light Bulb* (from *Death, Destruction, and Detroit*), 1979. Glass, metal, and neon

101. Robert Wilson, *Pierre Curie Chair*, 1989

102. Robert Wilson, *Parzival: a Chair with a Shadow*, 1987. Bleached birch with lacquer

103

The artist Ian Hamilton Finlay is best known for *Little Sparta,* an Arcadian installation and artist's residence he designed in the southern Highlands of Scotland. Within *Little Sparta,* Finlay combined traditional farm buildings, which the artist transformed into "temples," and works of art that are scattered and hidden among the classically designed gardens. The grounds and architecture convey the artist's continuing interest in the relationship between the real world and the cultural construct by which humans view their natural environment. Throughout the grounds, various quotations mounted on stone metaphorically draw attention to human interaction with, and intervention in, the landscape (fig. 103).

Born in the Bahamas, Finlay first gained recognition for his short stories, poems, and plays written in Scottish dialect, produced by the BBC in the 1950s. In the 1970s, he created works combining fragments of words with emblems of tanks, aircraft, and radar screens. Today, he is known for the diversity of his work: Finlay has also made prints, embroideries, landscape designs, and sculpture, many of which, while functional, are conceived as part of his art installations.

Much of Finlay's work has to do with the polarities between the natural and the cultivated, the present and the past, the land and the ocean. The sea has figured largely in Finlay's work (fig. 104), and it was the subject of his earliest sculptures from the 1960s and 1970s. In 1996, Finlay built a seaworthy "readymade" entitled *Dinghy* for exhibition at Tate St. Ives. On the wall facing the piece, the artist printed a diagrammatic "key" to identify its sections, and he also numbered those parts in paint directly on the small boat. As a result, the installation is not just offering a functional boat for our viewing, but also suggesting that viewers consider the elements involved in its construction. As the exhibition curator, Susan Daniel-McElroy, suggests, "It is a work in two clear parts. The real (boat) and the to-be-imagined (text) are set side-by-side—separate, but cross-referenced—and you are to feel their difference, their convergence."[1]

Since the late 1990s, Finlay has designed a series of wool blankets featuring minimal designs, colors, and diagrammatic text. In *Sails/Waves* (fig 105) the title words are written across the top and bottom of the left side respectively. Rippling waves punctuate the bottom third of the blanket, transformed up the right edge into an outline of billowing sails. Both waves and sails are provoked by the sea's winds. Without them, both are becalmed, their iconic lines flattened out.

103. Ian Hamilton Finlay,
Garden Seat, Little Sparta,
Dunsyre, Scotland

104. Ian Hamilton Finlay, *Wings*,
1997. Wood

105. Ian Hamilton Finlay,
Sails/Waves, 2001. Cashmere
and wool

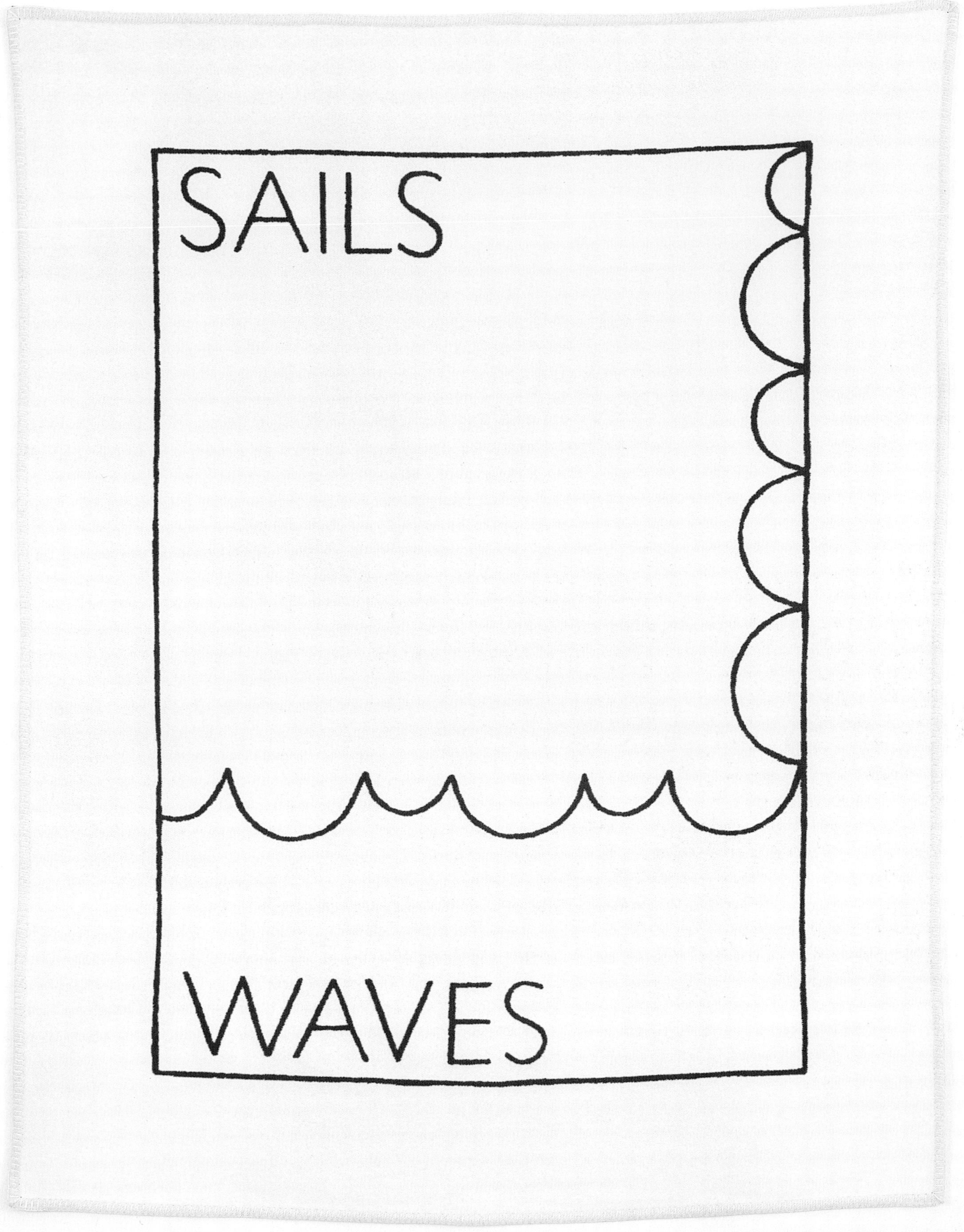
SAILS
WAVES

German-born Rosemarie Trockel has designed a number of ambiguous "functional" objects, including clothing, soup ladles, plates, stoves, mirrors, flocked wallpaper (fig. 107), and jewelry. Down comforters and pillows were the first works she sold at a small shop she and a partner owned in Cologne. In 1986, she designed a striped carpet, ceiling decorations, and a porcelain service for the ladies' drawing room in the German embassy in Washington, D.C.

Trockel discourages simplistic labeling of her work. She employs an array of materials in designing objects, and then has them produced, often using processes associated with gender, ethnography, commerce, and industry. Central to Trockel's vision is the idea of using fabric and knitting, with their traditionally feminine connotations, to explore systems that privilege the rational over the emotional and may be used to marginalize women and other cultures.

In the early 1980s, Trockel began knitting "pictures," supposedly as a reaction against critic Wolfgang M. Faust's disparaging remark that the only art women were capable of doing well was "weaving." The artist often incorporates, in serial form, icons and familiar logos, from the Playboy bunny to the hammer and sickle, integrated into the weaving of the material. Each of Trockel's knit works is designed on computer and manufactured according to the artist's instructions, offering a reference to Minimalist processes. However, at the same time, each work is unique, thereby subverting the premise of industrial production.

In 1986, Trockel produced a series of knitted *Balaklava* masks, like those worn by skiers in inclement weather—as well as by the terrorists responsible for the taking hostage of Israeli athletes at the Munich 1972 Olympics, which ended with the death of eleven members of the team (fig. 108). By exhibiting these functional objects within a museum case, the artist compels viewers to consider various contexts and associations they themselves bring to looking at these emotion-laden works. Trockel's strategy of reclassifying and recontextualizing functional objects that have intrinsic social and domestic associations recalls Duchamp's *Ready-mades* from the beginning of the century. The artist has repeated the plus-and-minus motif used on the *Balaklava* masks on a number of her other works, including several installations of a pair of asexual woolen leggings, with an opposing symbol on each leg. The arithmetic signs are also woven into Trockel's functional *Plus-Minus* (fig. 106), which forces users to make a conscious decision to stand either on the plus, or positive, side, or the less optimistic, and potentially destabilizing, minus portion.

In 1988, Trockel made a maquette entitled *Phobia*, which she said was "a commentary on the psychological classification of Donald Judd's attitude towards the female sex. Therefore I used an early photograph of Judd showing him contemplating his work, and I effeminized his haircut, the fly of his trousers, and the contour of his shirt."[1] She subsequently made another Judd-related work, *Phobia 2002,* in which five horizontal metal panels are placed, like a Judd stack, on a wall. Each of the industrial metal components is "accessorized" with a black fringe, thereby feminizing Judd's austere work.

Most recently, in collaboration with artist Carsten Hoeller, Trockel has designed "utopian animal shelters," including *A House for Pigs and People,* which was exhibited at *Documenta* in 1997. Throughout her career, Trockel has resisted categorizing her work as either masterpiece or mundane, conceptual art or design. Rather, she collects, researches, edits, and remixes socially defined materials, and asks us to reconsider the implicit messages they convey.

107

106. Rosemarie Trockel, *Plus-Minus*, 1987. Hand-knotted wool. Produced by Equator Productions, New York

107. Rosemarie Trockel, *Eiwess* flocked wallpaper, 1998

108. Rosemarie Trockel, *Balaklava* (two versions), 1986. Wool

While acknowledging that "I am certainly a by-product of Judd doing what he did, or I wouldn't be what I am," Barbara Bloom nevertheless emphatically states, "it is not where I am today, and it is far from anything that now interests me."[1] Rather than make austere pieces, Bloom creates obsessive, object-rich installations where everything is considered and designed in detail. She considers her work, although formed from recognizable objects, as abstract triggers for thinking, particularly about ethical and philosophical issues.

The creation of Bloom's work, in such installations as *The Reign of Narcissism* (fig. 109) or *The French Diplomat's Office,* requires that the artist conduct extensive research in a range of disciplines, including ethnography, biography, geology, history, anthropology, literature, and art history. For Bloom, it does not matter whether the elements she includes in the final work are considered art objects or not. She is far more interested in the ideas, events, and associations they elicit, the metaphoric connections they educe with adjacent objects, and the new ideas and relationships formed in viewers' minds as a result of extended viewing. Bloom wants to provoke her audience to look at the world differently, so that, for instance, after seeing a cup in one of her installations, they reconsider the form, style, and implications of all the drinking containers they use in daily life.

In 1999, on the centennial of writer Vladimir Nabokov's birth, Bloom was asked to design an exhibition of his library (fig. 110). Reflecting Nabokov's fascination with butterflies and their sexual interplay, Bloom displayed his extensive book collections within large, glazed butterfly cases. One small room was filled with the covers of numerous translations of Nabokov's celebrated novel *Lolita*. Bloom designed the wallpaper with reproductions of the drawings, notes, and annotations that cover his manuscripts and novels. To further the sense of the visitor being inside Nabokov's mind, Bloom designed a rug for the floor (fig. 111). Its minimal design is taken directly from Nabokov's first edition of *Lolita*, a book initially deemed pornographic and banned in the United States. The rug's imagery replicates the book's cover exactly. Bordered with bands of black and white, the title lettering spreads across the top third of the rug's face, with the name of the publisher, The Olympia Press, at the bottom. The carpet carries rich and complex metaphoric associations, including issues of ownership, reproduction, and translation.

Often, after designing an installation, Bloom decides that certain parts or objects from the whole can stand on their own as icons containing the essential ideas of the exhibition. Bloom has taken a number of these objects, like the *Lolita* rug, and had them produced as functional editions so that they are more accessible. The carpet was produced in an edition of ten, and the artist expressly wants people to use it, stating, "I like the patina of use, showing that there have been people walking on and around the work."[2]

Because she carefully researches and considers every aspect of every installation, Bloom feels that her function as an artist "is not that different from that of a designer, except that I am giving the design problems and challenges to *myself*, rather than getting them from a client or functional need. I do go about the design and making with a similar practical sense of the designer, and I enjoy that process very much."

109. Barbara Bloom, *The Reign of Narcissism*, 1988–89. Mixed-media installation

110. Barbara Bloom, installation view, *Revised Evidence: Vladimir Nabokov's Inscriptions, Annotations, Corrections, and Butterfly Descriptions*, Glen Horowitz Bookseller, New York, 1999

111. Barbara Bloom, *Lolita*, 1999. Wool

Although there are significant differences between Dan Flavin's and Donald Judd's work, Flavin's initial "Minimalist" pieces also evolved from his early experiments with painting and found materials, and from his desire to break away from the hegemony of traditional art forms. Like Judd and Burton, Flavin was keenly interested throughout his career in the integration of art with architecture. However, in all of his efforts, the architectural context and ambient light are integral to their viewing, and signal a new approach to, and form of, creative work. Flavin's work reflects a synthesis of Judd's use of industrial materials (the objectness of the lights themselves) and Burton's emphasis on the *experiential* nature of the best art. Even Flavin's porcelain plates, among the only purely functional works he designed, share basic affinities with his light works in their focus on light diffusion and radiating color, and the necessity for interaction with the surrounding space in order to be properly "seen."

Flavin was born in Queens, New York, and attended a Catholic seminary before training in meteorology in the Air Force. Returning to the city in 1956, Flavin attended the New School and Columbia University, where he studied painting, art history, and literature. In 1961, he began working on "plain, physical, factual paintings of firm plasticity in opposition to the loose, vacuous . . . fantasies . . . of a declining generation." Combining geometric-shaped Masonite boxes raised several inches from the wall with various types of attached lights, Flavin created a series of hybrid works. He titled these *icons* to dissociate them, as Judd did, from traditional painting or sculpture.

The *icons* were intended to be shown in groups, so that the illumination of each would interact with others in the series. Judd reviewed an exhibition of Flavin's *icons*, calling the show "one of the most interesting I've seen this year. . . . There are several interesting aspects to the pieces: they are things themselves, they are awkward; they are put together bluntly, the materials are considered bluntly — the paint is flat and the lights come that way; the lights are strong and specific."[1] In 1962, Flavin designed *icon V (Coran's Broadway Flesh)* (fig. 113), a square of Masonite, painted bright red, and surrounded on all four sides by incandescent, "candle-shaped" bulbs. Like Judd, he was not interested in conveying spiritual or transcendent associations through these works, but in exploring perception — how the use of light affects the experience of seeing.

Over the next few years, Flavin moved away from making discrete objects, preferring instead to use the qualities of light to dematerialize solid forms and surrounding architecture. Flavin's artist-designed *icons*, with their incandescent light, gave way to the incorporation of non-artist-mediated, commercially available fixtures and industrial lighting, recalling Marcel Duchamp's *Ready-mades*.[2] In May 1963, Flavin placed a white fluorescent light tube diagonally on a wall. Subtitled *To Constantin Brancusi*, this was Flavin's first fully mature fluorescent work, and it represented his final break with traditional art forms (fig. 114). As Flavin's work evolved, it increased in complexity via three central elements: the use of standardized fluorescent tubes and fittings (thereby abandoning any reference to the subjective gesture of Abstract Expressionism); the simple, often serially repetitive arrangement and placement of the tubes and their fixtures; and the ambient, luminous nature of the light itself as it affected the surrounding space.

By 1969, Judd was contrasting his work and Flavin's, noting, "I want a particular definite object. I think Flavin wants, at least first or primarily, a particular phenomenon."[3] (Fig. 115) As the effects of his light works became more subtle and complex, Flavin moved away from his contemporaries' definitions of art as "specific objects" or "primary structures." Instead, the works literally dissolved architecture. As Flavin noted, "I knew that the actual space of a room could be broken down and played with by planting illusions of real light, electric light, at crucial junctures in the room's composition . . . you can destroy that corner by glare and double shadow."[4]

By the 1970s, Flavin turned toward larger-scale and architectural installations. In 1971, he was invited to mount an exhibition of his work along the circular, interior ramps of the Solomon R. Guggenheim Museum's Frank Lloyd Wright building in New York (fig. 118 shows the exhibition as reinstalled in 1992). By situating his fluorescent lights strategically along the rounded walls leading up to the dome, Flavin created an installation of extraordinary, mesmerizing rings of brilliant, palpable color that highlighted the overall beauty of the architecture. Each floor glowed with refulgent hues, emphasizing the bands between them like stacked dishes. Through their center, from the dome to the floor, the artist extended a column of layered white fluorescent tubes. In 1972, Flavin similarly

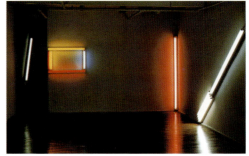

112. Dan Flavin, *Untitled*, Santa Maria in Chiesa Rossa, Milan, Italy, 1996. Blue, green, yellow, and filtered U.V. fluorescent light

113. Dan Flavin, *icon V (Coran's Broadway Flesh)*, 1962. Oil on Masonite and clear, incandescent lightbulbs

114. Dan Flavin, *Untitled (To Constantin Brancusi)*, 1963. White fluorescent light

115. Dan Flavin, *Fluorescent Light*, 1964, installation view, Green Gallery, New York

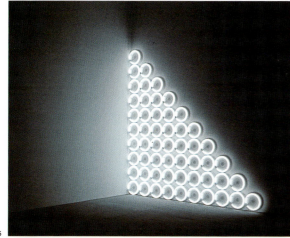

116

117

116. Dan Flavin, *Untitled (To a Man, George McGovern)*, 1972. Warm-white fluorescent light

117. Dan Flavin, Chinati Foundation installation, Marfa, TX, 1996–2000

118. Dan Flavin, *Untitled (To Tracy, for the Love of a Lifetime)*, 1992. Fluorescent light fixture with pink lamps

119. Dan Flavin, *For André Raynaud*, 1990. Porcelain

installed *Untitled (To a Man, George McGovern)*, a series of fifty-five circular, white fluorescent rings lined up and ascending a wall, in the home of Philippa and Heiner Frederich of the Dia Center for the Arts. Forming an equilateral triangle, they cast a glowing light on the wall that was reflected across the adjacent floor (fig. 116).

In 1990, in a manner similar to his Guggenheim and Frederich installations, Flavin designed a plate service containing six place settings of five dishes each. He titled these functional porcelain plates *For André Raynaud* (fig. 119). When seen in the proper light, the dishes recall Maurice Merleau-Ponty's observations on experience: "At those times when we allow ourselves simply to be in the world without actively assuming it . . . different planes are no longer distinguishable, and colors are no longer condensed into superficial colors, but are diffused round about objects and become atmospheric colors."[5] The plates, which Flavin produced in an edition of 150, consist of thin, white, delicately shaped porcelain. The artist designed these both to be used and as a study of reflectivity and the aura of light in different contexts. To this end, he covered the underside of each plate in the graduated stacks with a thick coat of one of five rich, vibrant primary colors. When used singly, the plates' undercoat is barely visible—just as a Flavin light work, when turned off, appears to be a mere unused light fixture.[6] When the plates are stacked, however, particularly on a white surface or tablecloth, the under-painting of the upper plate suffuses the porcelain surface below with reflected color. The artist did not design cups to accompany the plates, as the color would by necessity have to be plainly visible on the outside surface, and that didn't interest him. Instead, for Flavin, the "magic" of the work was in the reflected light.

Just as with the enormous works Flavin installed between 1996 and 2000 at Judd's Chinati Foundation in Marfa (fig. 117), the "light" and colors radiating off Flavin's functional porcelain plates cannot be captured physically. His works are purely perceptual experiences, whether they fill a room with light, give particular character to an architectural site, or simply add a visual experience to the act of setting a table. For Flavin, the question of whether his creations are art or design, or even architecture, is largely moot, and any answer is as ephemeral and phenomenological as the works themselves.

The Guggenheim Museum and the Art of this Century

James Turrell has consistently defied any attempt to label or categorize any of his work. From small holograms to his transformation of a volcano in Arizona into spaces for perception, Turrell's intention is to make viewers physically conscious of the experience of seeing. Furthermore, one cannot define his work according to traditional media, as his is more the creation of architectural/perceptual conditions than of specific objects. His work is variously described as "viewing chambers where seeing takes place,"[1] and as "shelves" into which viewers look and explore the quality of light and space. In essence, Turrell makes work in which he exchanges light for paint, wood, and other conventional art-making materials.

Although his "material" is light, there is an inherent difference between Turrell's work and that of Flavin, who used commercial fluorescent light tubes to emphasize the physicality of light fixtures as objects. For Turrell, the main interest is in the visual dissolution of any architectural or structural constraints. In his work, light has its own presence, rather than being something by which you illuminate something else. "The space, then, is emptied out to become a place of withdrawal and immanence concerning the gaze itself: *a looking into*," as Turrell puts it, opposed to any vision in quest of an object (*a looking at*).[2] In addition, Turrell creates spaces that "relate to what they really are, that is, light resting in a space."[3] Unlike Minimalist tenets that stressed the literal, rejecting illusion, Turrell embraces it, remarking, "I like illusion when it is so convincing that we might as well see reality this way—I like to present to our belief system something that is convincing, that 'we know not to be.'"[4]

In his early works, such as *Afrum I* (fig. 121), Turrell projected an illusory cube of light against the corner of a room, with the result that the glowing form actually appears to hang in space. Describing this work as being like little "holes in reality,"[5] Turrell continued to pursue the creation of forms the identity of which is a function of the viewer's changing perspective through movement. Turrell's early *Skyscapes*, such as *Meeting* (fig. 122), involved cutting a rectangle through the ceiling, leaving the room open to the sky. The artist describes his intention as wanting to give viewers the feeling that they were "sensing" space: "I try to take light and materialize it in its physical aspects so you really feel it— feel the physicality."[6] When, in the early 1990s, Turrell turned to designing functional objects, this language of light remained a central principle.

In 1993, Turrell visited a country-house museum in Leeds, England, where he was particularly drawn to a set of Josiah Wedgwood's black basalt ware (also called Quaker ware). The work reminded him of the ceramics he encountered growing up in a Quaker community in California (fig. 123). Five years later, working with Irish potter Nicholas Mosse—who, like Turrell, considers himself a lapsed Quaker—the artist designed his version of functional basalt ware in various austere, Neo-classical, black and white shapes, many reminiscent of traditional Wedgwood designs. Turrell and Mosse's *Lapsed Quaker Ware* was first installed in a Quaker school in Yorkshire, England, in 1998. Subsequently, the edition of more than seventy ceramics has been exhibited on its own, and as arranged on the shelves of a Shaker-style sideboard, hanging cabinet, and table, designed by Turrell and made by cabinetmaker William Burke (fig. 120).

As in the case of so many of Turrell's installations, when the basalt ware is installed in the cherry wood furniture, viewers have to look *into* the space to see the pieces. "You have this preloading in the way of setting someone up for the experience to come—whether it's just with dark adaptation, the time to let the eye open, or whether it is loading with a certain color. . . . By giving it time there is discovery . . . this revelation that isn't given all at once."[7] Partially shrouded in shadow, the obsidian ceramics initially appear as flat, abstract shapes until the viewer's eye gradually adjusts to their three-dimensional form. Ironically, in opposition to Turrell's other works, the ceramics eclipse light, and thwart perception. Their matte surfaces literally swallow light, making it necessary to come close to the objects in order to see them properly. Once in close proximity, the works reveal that what appear to be pitch-black surfaces are, in fact, incised with concentric ring decoration (fig. 124). As Brooks Adams observed, "Each of the plates, tankards, and bowls has a whirring kind of stillness: the plates seem to roil quietly in their empty centers and then take off in the striated 'rays' and combined 'waves' of their borders."[8]

Turrell's basalt ware and Shaker-style furniture address issues of light and perception that the artist investigated in his earlier work, and that he is continuing to examine in his ongoing project: the monumental *Roden Crater* in northern Arizona. The concentric rings incised in the *Lapsed Quaker Ware* surfaces resemble the furrowed surfaces of the volcano as seen from aerial photographs,

120. James Turrell/William Burke, *Lapsed Quaker Ware*, installation view, A/D Gallery, New York, 1998

121. James Turrell, *Afrum I*, 1967. Xenon projection

122. James Turrell, *Meeting*, 1980–86. Interior tungsten light and open sky. Permanent installation, P.S. 1, New York

121

122

and the controlled tunneling through the bowels of the mountain. Like the geologic processes of the volcano, the ceramics are made from natural materials that are subjected to extreme heat and, as a result, are fundamentally transformed. Both Turrell's "art" and his functional objects engage perceptual phenomena to direct viewers' attention toward questions concerning the nature of light, space, and time.

Recently, Turrell has taken on a number of architectural projects, including designing the interior of a Quaker meeting house in Texas, a screening room in a private home in California, and all of the furniture for the guest lodge nestled on the south side of the Roden Crater. Each project involves viewer participation in prolonged, dedicated looking. Like so much of the work using minimal materials and lacking narrative, there is an implied contradiction in Turrell's work: its initial perceived simplicity forces close, active, prolonged, even "maximal" looking in order to perceive its complexity.

Whether his work is described as art, installation, or architecture, Turrell continues to challenge viewers to be more conscious of how we see, what we see, and how we fit in the larger world. As he expresses it, "My desire is to set up a situation to which I take you and let you see. It becomes your experience."[9]

123

123. Josiah Wedgwood & Sons, black basalt ware, c. 1775–1800

124. James Turrell, *Lapsed Quaker Ware*, detail, 1998. Black basalt

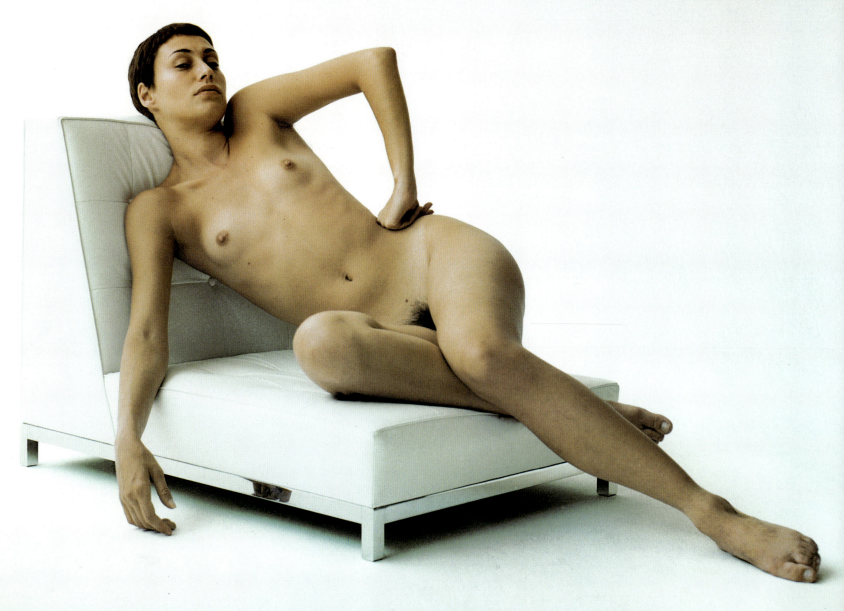

Provocateur Tom Sachs calls himself an artisan, noting, "I'm an artist because my career as a carpenter was unsuccessful."[1] Sachs spent two years at the Architectural Association in London before working for furniture company Knoll, designer Tom Dixon, and architect Frank Gehry (on his hockey-stick furniture). In 1994, Sachs was hired by Barney's to decorate its Madison Avenue store's holiday windows. Several of these, such as his Christmas nativity scene with three Bart Simpson figures as the Magi and Hello Kitty as the baby Jesus, caused a furor. In his ongoing sculpture and installations, Sachs continually mixes idioms, such as his incorporation of found objects like telephone books and parking meters into bases for lamps (fig. 126). He also recasts objects of consumer "lust and desire" by contextualizing and building, with mundane materials, everyday functional objects—toilets with the Prada imprimatur or skateboards with a swastika and Burberry patterns—into elegant icons of status and prestige (fig. 127).

Also in 1994, Sachs designed a to-scale cardboard prototype for a piece of furniture that he titled *Bitch Lounge.* The work was then put into production under the auspices of *nest* magazine (fig. 125).[2] Sachs's "anti-couch" contains many elements that reflect the artist's keen interest in the history of Modernist design. Like Mies van der Rohe's *Barcelona Chair*, *Bitch Lounge* is upholstered in carefully considered, tufted leather and mounted on a chrome-plated steel base. Sachs took a great deal of care and interest in the details of the chair's construction, including the density of the foam, the curve of the back, and the placement of the buttons. Despite being produced as a fully functional piece of furniture, Sachs's seat is singularly uncomfortable and difficult to use. Barely raised off the ground, the lounge does not allow the sitter to "sit" conventionally without bending his or her legs so they sit directly under the chin, or having to extend them horizontally (fig. 128).

Sachs's work is often referred to as "bricolage," connoting something that is put together using whatever materials happen to be available, rather than procuring them specifically for a piece or project. When asked whether he makes any distinction today between art and design, his answer is characteristically enigmatic: "If it doesn't look good no one will want to look at it. The distinction between artist and engineer is humiliating. Artists make crippled furniture and functional art."[3]

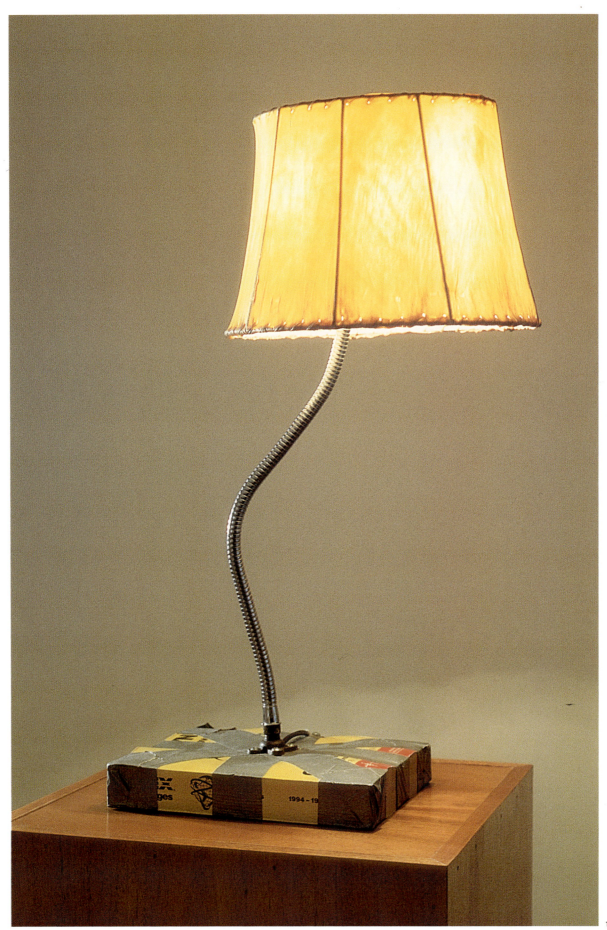

125. Tom Sachs, *Bitch Lounge* with nude, *nest* magazine, 1999

126. Tom Sachs, *Untitled (Telephone Lamp)*, 1994. Telephone book, duct tape, flexible metal stem, and electric cord

127. Tom Sachs, *Prada Toilet*, 1997. Cardboard and glue

128. Tom Sachs, *Bitch Lounge*, 1999. Welded, chrome-plated steel base with tufted leather upholstery

Rachel Whiteread acknowledges that she was influenced by the language, scale, and "freshness" of American Minimalism of the mid-twentieth century, particularly in the primacy it attached to simple materials, the lack of visible gesture, and the importance of space. As she recalls, "Minimalism was definitely an influence, as it gave me the confidence to place something in the middle of the floor and let it be what it was."[1] In her work, such as cast-resin water towers, and plaster casts of the space around buildings, bookshelves, and the negative space created under chairs and tables, she has devised a new idiom of form, and forced an innovative way of viewing the world.

During the mid-1980s in London, Whiteread began making casts of parts of her body. Although she never publicly exhibited this work, she turned a casting of her back into a functional shovel, reminiscent of Duchamp's *In Advance of the Broken Arm.* Intrigued by the idea of objects having a human presence, Whiteread began making plaster and resin casts of used furniture and ordinary domestic objects. In order to de-familiarize these objects, Whiteread employed the traditional techniques of casting. She is not as interested in casting the actual object as she is in concretizing the negative space around it. This recalls Burton's desire to create art that places itself "not in front of, but around, behind, underneath (literally) the audience." To manifest the usually invisible, Whiteread uses an array of materials, including plaster, concrete, resin, and rubber.

Like Artschwager, Whiteread considers furniture and its forms and connotations as the starting point for much of her artwork of the last decade and a half. As she acknowledges, she uses "furniture as a metaphor for human beings."[2] In 1988, for her first gallery exhibition, Whiteread bought three pieces of used furniture—a dressing table, a wardrobe, and a bed—and filled them with wet plaster, removing the wood when it had set. What remained were the spaces in between and around the furniture. As the artist noted, "The first table I made . . . was to do with exchanging one's personal space with that of that table, the physicality of how you sit when you have a table in front of you, how your legs behave."[3] Whiteread has since cast beds, baths, sinks, floors, whole rooms, and building exteriors in plaster, rubber, and wax. Her work makes the negative space—the container of memories—visible (fig. 130). By casting from specific objects, Whiteread is able to capture the marks of "the life in which they had a function." In casting a used table that was

similar to one in her grandmother's kitchen, for example, the final cast included vestiges of "all sorts of bits and horrible stuff that you find beneath tables."[4]

In 1991, Whiteread reproduced the underside of a bed in rubber (fig. 131). Flexible enough to bend and "give," it would, ostensibly, still function. However, she placed it partially against a wall, thereby animating the wall and forcing viewers to consider the result as a sculpture. "Slumped up against the wall, I would see it out of the corner of my eye and it was like a person. Kind of forgotten about and left in a corner."[5] In 1996, Whiteread cast the space underneath ten generic tables in order to create *Untitled (Ten Tables)*. Once the original forms were cut away, all that remained was a newly visible, palpable memory of the originals.

Recently, the artist became interested in going outside of the studio and creating work that referenced her sculpture, but was not as "precious." She chose a daybed as the form from which to make her first functional edition. As she recalls, "I wanted to make something that had to be furniture." For Whiteread, the daybed represents a "resting spot, a pause," both figuratively from her usual activity of art-making, and literally as a place for users to stop and unwind. Combining ideas from several of her rubber and plaster sculptures, she conceived of *Daybed* (fig. 129) as having a form that would "entice you to lay on it but it is

129. Rachel Whiteread, Allison Harbertson with *Daybed, in situ* in private home, New York, 2003

130. Rachel Whiteread, *Untitled (Black Bed)*, 1991. Rubber

131. Rachel Whiteread, *Untitled (Amber Bed)*, 1991. Rubber

132. Rachel Whiteread, *Daybed*, 1999. Beech wood and multi density foams with wool upholstery

132

not really that comfortable."[6] Whiteread intended *Daybed* to mimic, but not be an exact prototype of, her sculptures (fig. 132). With her assistants, Whiteread made the first to-scale model in wood, taking the piece apart five times in order to ensure that the "upholstered holes" at each corner went straight through the form to the ground. As it was to be a functional object, the artist found she had to consider mundane matters, such as ensuring a child's hand could not get stuck in the holes. As she notes, this was a different process from creating her artworks, as she "really enjoyed being forced to think of such practical things for a change."

Whiteread's *Daybed* is very similar to the one she remembers from her parents' home. Adding another layer of meaning to the work, the fabric the artist chose for her prototype *Daybed*, a dusty gray in color, is a facsimile of the one in her memory. As the artist acknowledges of *Daybed* and her other, non-functional work, "There are all sorts of stories related to the pieces I make . . . it is inevitable that the history of objects becomes a part of the work."[7] Admitting that she would like to design functional work again, Whiteread notes, "I think the thing that interests me most in furniture is getting it out into domestic environments— that the work has another life altogether than my sculpture. I want to continue making things that are 'outward' in the world and accessible to more people."[8]

Cuban-born Jorge Pardo's works are always conceived in relation to architecture and to their surroundings. The dual nature of his work, as art and as functional design, should perhaps be referred to by a new label such as "art practice," rather than by either of the traditional terms. Unlike Judd, Pardo rejects seeing the results of his efforts as purely objective; instead, he accepts the subjective associations viewers make in their perception of the work. He often infuses unusually brilliant colors into his architectural installations, giving them a sense of animation and optimism (fig. 133). Pardo covered the first floor of the Dia Center for the Arts in New York—9000 square feet (840 m²) of floor and walls—with bright yellow, orange, gray, and green ceramic tiles, and designed new seating and shelving systems for the space. Rather than just designing a space, Pardo also designed related furniture and paintings, allowing visitors to examine how they distinguish between what is commonly considered art and how they define design.

The artist often refers to his Los Angeles home, which he designed and titled *4166 Sea View Lane,* as a sculpture. After its completion, he opened the house to the public for six weeks. The interior features Pardo's 1950s- and 1960s-inspired furniture and lamps that rely on placement and interaction for proper viewing. Christopher Knight of the *Los Angeles Times* noted, "Pardo's remarkable house . . . further extends a defining artistic tradition in postwar L.A. . . . questioning the conventions that typically separate art and craft, or gratuitous aesthetic inquiry from the functional demands of utilitarian objects."[1]

In 1990, Pardo used welded copper pipes to design the singularly uncomfortable *Le Corbusier Chair* (fig. 134). The artist has also designed several series of lights that offer amusing suggestions of what might have happened had Noguchi and a manufacturer of hard candy collaborated on designs. One, a tri-part hanging installation, is made of glass forms, alternately colored lemon-yellow, butterscotch, and blood-red. Meanwhile, his grouping of glass floor lamps crouches on the ground like radiant, psychedelic mushrooms (fig. 135). As Pardo demonstrates, art and functional work can not only be interrelated in terms of design, but also form a new category of object, all the while—like Tuttle's work—infusing daily life with humor.

133. Jorge Pardo, *Project*, 2000.
Three parts: lobby, bookshop,
and gallery, commissioned by
the Dia Center for the Arts,
New York

134. Jorge Pardo, *Le Corbusier
Chair*, 1990. Welded copper pipes

135. Jorge Pardo, *Untitled (Floor
Lamps)*, 2003. Glass

Like Scott Burton decades earlier, Austrian artist Franz West conflates art and design by making virtually all of his work functional and interactive. By producing objects and installations that are accessible and by inviting their active exploitation, West forces viewers to consider the usefulness of art and the potentially transformative qualities of furniture through innovative behavior.

West's early work, known as "Fitting Pieces," were intended to be selected, worn, and carried around by viewers so that each person became an active part of the whole. He first achieved public recognition for his collages and assembled papier-mâché sculptures. These were often painted in vibrant colors (particularly pink, which the artist considers "the color of happiness") (fig. 137). West was influenced early in his career by Richard Artschwager's work, and his experimentation with concepts of art and design. As West recalls, "I thought to myself, it's good that you can sit on it."[1] As a result, West began designing a number of eccentric, oddly shaped objects, and experimental furniture that he covered and bound with different materials, such as collage, bandages, and papier-mâché, noting, "I do furniture, I like to do it myself, not ready-mades. . . . To me, it is like body training, like exercise."[2]

West subsequently designed a number of sculptures that could be positioned according to the whim of the audience. In so doing, he relinquished control over the work and invited viewers to sit, socialize, and become part of his furniture/sculpture. As he stated, "I want the artwork to be real . . . to be able to step into it, to sit on it, to lie on it . . . this is the art of today, lying down on the bed looking up into space. It doesn't matter what the art looks like but how it's used."[3] Without some functionality, or what he calls "active reception," West believes that anything "remain[s] somehow wanting, unfulfilled . . . the equivalent of a lack." As a result, West encourages participants to "go ahead"[4] and interact with the materials.

In 1994, West created *Rest* (fig. 136), a site-specific installation of twenty-seven welded-steel couches and tables on the rooftop at the Dia Center for the Arts in New York. The simple metal-framed furniture was covered with bold black-and-white patterned fabric made by fellow artist Gilvert Bretterbauer. Visitors were invited to spend time socializing on the couches. West occasionally invited fellow artists to "curate" his work, and, with collaborators, he designed very basic welded and wood furniture, including frames for a number of benches, chairs, tables, and couches. In some cases, the seats of these pieces were covered with newspaper so that the ink rubbed off on users' clothes, as evidence of the work's functionality.

Literally and conceptually, West's work *Creativity* offers the perfect dénouement for the "dialogue" among the works in *Design ≠ Art,* as it leaves the question of any differentiation between the two up to the visitor. Like so much of West's work, *Creativity* (fig. 138) is predicated on the artist's total rejection of art's usual privileging of primary authorship: the rudimentary table, chairs, and lamp arrive ready to be assembled and positioned by the recipient. Included in the crate is a large box containing variously colored rolls of masking tape. Once the work is placed in a room, West invites viewers to take pieces of the primary colored tape and use it to drape, cover, bind, and transform the wood and metal surfaces of the furniture in any configuration they wish. Any visitor or passerby is invited to add a small mark of color or stretch huge strips of tape around entire sections of the furniture. As a result, unless one runs out of tape, the work is never "finished" or fully "designed."

Creativity also raises provocative questions in keeping with the wide-ranging views on the differences between art and design held by many of the artists in *Design ≠ Art*. For example, if an artist visiting an exhibition decides to add some tape to West's *Creativity*, does that make it more of an "artwork" than if a casual visitor augments it? Would authorship then have to be shared between the artist and West as collaborators? And what if a child stretches tape around the table, so that the legs were completely bound, thereby making the table unusable? Would the now "functionless" table be more of an art installation than furniture? In *Creativity*, as with the work of so many of the artists today, the differentiation between design and art remains fluid and unresolved.

137

136. Franz West, *Rest,* 1994, installation view, Dia Center for the Arts, New York. Twenty-seven welded-steel couches and accompanying tables

137. Franz West, installation view, *Sisyphus: Litter and Waste* exhibition, featuring *Corona,* enamel on aluminum, orange couch, and two collages, Gagosian Gallery, New York, 2002

138. Franz West, *Creativity: Furniture Reversal,* 1998. Two chairs, table, lamp, and colored duct tape

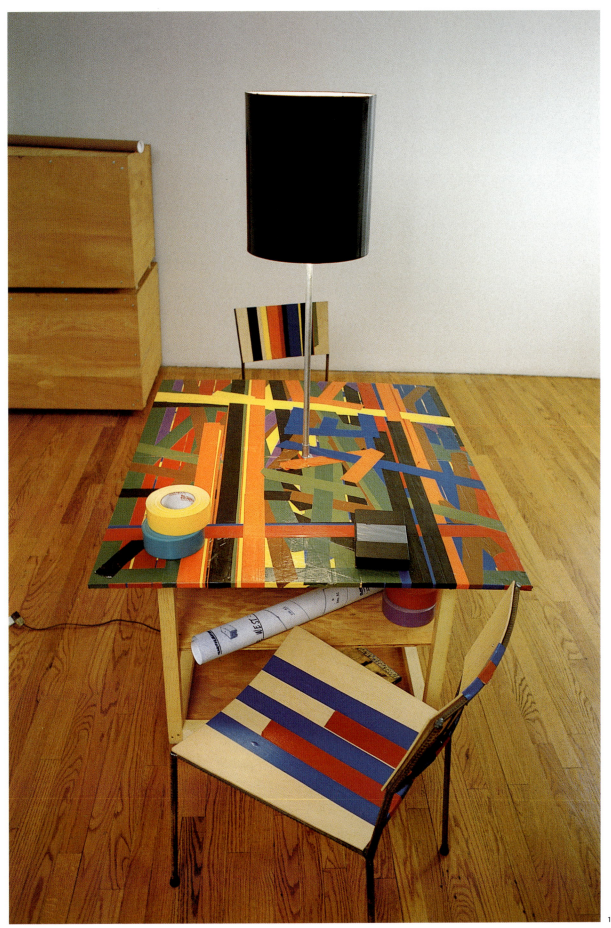

The works of the artists in *Design ≠ Art*, while visually very different, demonstrate a serious commitment to both art and design, and to maintaining some tension between the two. Although a few voiced strong, polarized opinions on the difference and hierarchy by which we should consider art and design, most of the artists' opinions and functional works fall somewhere on the continuum between the two extreme positions taken by Donald Judd and Scott Burton. While some of the artists presented here have designed limited functional pieces, others have made large quantities of furniture and decorative arts, always concurrently with their artwork. In addition, many plan to continue or resume designing functional work in the future.

The early 1960s offered artists searching for a new paradigm unique opportunities to explore, identify, and define what art could be, using what later came to be known as "Minimalism" as a starting point. As Western economies prospered, the contemporary art market expanded, fueled by the perceived prestige granted to the elite who understood and collected the most innovative works of art. As a result, the financial stakes increased exponentially. As the second half of the twentieth century progressed, the media increasingly bestowed celebrity on notable and noted artists. This was particularly true in the United States, where design and functional work continued, until very recently, to play a supporting role to fine art's lead. Given the economic inequalities between the support for fine art and design, there was little incentive for artists who were also designing functional works to market the furniture and objects they designed.

Today, however, the rigid aesthetic hierarchy has broken down as works by an increasing number of international designers command a higher price tag than many of their fellow artists' work. Design is in the ascendant, and is globally recognized as a singularly important conveyer of personal and cultural expression. During this time of aesthetic pluralism, it is therefore appropriate to revisit and celebrate openly the little-known design works by the artists described in this book. As George Kubler suggested forty years ago, trying to define the differences between art and design equitably and conclusively is meaningless, as "the pure extremes are only in our imagination: human products always incorporate both utility and art in varying mixtures, and no object is conceivable without the admixture of both." As Kubler proposes, like the artists whose work reflects a synthesis, perhaps we should instead consider reuniting both art and functional design under the rubric of visual forms, so that "the idea of art . . . be expanded to embrace the whole range of man-made things, including all . . . the useless, beautiful, and poetic things of the world. . . . From all these things, a shape in time emerges. A visible portrait of the collective identity . . . comes into being . . . and it eventually becomes the portrait given to posterity."[1]

In the twenty-first century, design may not be exactly the same as art, but neither is it—nor should it be—considered a lesser cultural form. At a time characterized by diversity and the dissolution of confining boundaries, it is worth reconsidering what Richard Tuttle gleefully refers to as one of the "great secrets of the twentieth century": the functional objects designed by artists from Donald Judd to Rachel Whiteread. At the very least, as Tuttle suggests, these thought-provoking works show that there are more varieties of human creative output than we have defined categories within which to consign them, a fact that should both surprise and give us pleasure. As he further observes in terms of differentiating art and design, "I have no answers or declarations—questions are, however, always appropriate."[2]

139. Donald Judd, *Desk with Two Chairs #97*, 1992. Fin color plywood

140. Donald Judd, *Chairs #84/85*, 1987 (two of a set of ten variations). Fin color plywood

JOHN CHAMBERLAIN

1. Telephone interview with the artist, October 29, 2003.

2. Donald Judd, "In the Galleries," *Arts Magazine*, March 1962, p. 46.

3. Donald Judd, "In the Galleries," *Arts Magazine*, February 1960, p. 10.

4. Donald Judd, "Christmas–New Year: 1963–4," *Art International*, December 1963, reprinted in Judd, *Complete Writings*, 1975, p. 109.

5. John Chamberlain, quotes from 1982, printed on Chamberlain flyer at the Chinati Foundation, Marfa, TX.

6. Leo Castelli was Chamberlain's dealer and a highly influential gallerist and promoter of contemporary art.

7. Telephone interview with the artist, October 29, 2003.

8. *Ibid.*

9. Domergue 1984, p. 62. (Special thanks to Nathan Joseph for allowing us to use in the *Design ≠ Art* exhibition sections of the film he made during his visit to Chamberlain's studio while Chamberlain was "carving" his foam couches.)

10. Telephone conversation with the author, November 2003.

RICHARD ARTSCHWAGER

1. Conversation with the artist, September 25, 2003, New York.

2. Richard Artschwager, quoted in Naylor and P-Orridge 1977, p. 46.

3. Conversation with the artist, January 10, 2004, New York.

4. Conversation with the artist, September 25, 2003, New York.

5. Artschwager's comment on Formica is quoted in Jan McDevitt, "The Object: Still Life, Interviews with New Object Makers, Richard Artschwager and Claes Oldenburg, on Craftsmanship, Art and Function," *Craft Horizons* 25, September–October 1965, p. 30. Judd reviewed Artschwager's work, noting that it "purposely resembles furniture" and stating his preference for one of the artist's desks, as its "obscurity of reference and plainness are better than the obvious reference and partitioning of the other pieces." Donald Judd, "In the Galleries," *Arts Magazine*, March 1965, reprinted in Judd, *Complete Writings*, 1975, p. 167.

6. Domergue 1984, p. 47; and conversation with the artist, September 25, 2003, New York.

7. Ingrid Schaffner, "The Curious Case of the DOOR MIRROR BASKET RUG TABLE WINDOW," in Artschwager 1998, p. 29.

8. Domergue 1984, p. 47.

9. Conversation with the artist, September 25, 2003, New York.

10. *Ibid.*

11. Richard Artschwager, quoted in Adrian Searle, "No Function Required," *The Guardian*, December 18, 2001.

12. Conversation with the artist, January 10, 2004, New York.

13. Conversation with the artist, September 25, 2003, New York; with additional quote from an interview between the artist and Brooke Alexander in fall 1990, cited in Alexander 1991.

14. Conversation with the artist, September 25, 2003, New York.

SOL LEWITT

1. Sol LeWitt, "Paragraphs on Conceptual Art," *Artforum* 5, no. 10, June 1967, pp. 79–83, reprinted in Garrels 2000, p. 369.

2. Sol LeWitt, "Sentences on Conceptual Art, 1968," in Meyer 1972, p. 175. Also reprinted in Sol LeWitt, "Sentences on Conceptual Art, " *Art-Language* 1, no. 1, May 1969, pp. 11–13.

3. Sol LeWitt, "Paragraphs on Conceptual Art," *Artforum* 5, no. 10, June 1967, pp. 79–83.

4. LeWitt quoted in "Beauty and the Brain," on-line article by Glen Helfand, *San Francisco Bay Guardian*, February 16, 2000 (http://www.sfbg.com/AandE/34/20/lead.html), active April 5, 2004.

5. *Ibid.*

6. Domergue 1984, p. 107.

7. Sol LeWitt, "Paragraphs on Conceptual Art," *Artforum* 5, no. 10, June 1967, pp. 79–83, reprinted in Garrels 2000, p. 370.

JOEL SHAPIRO

1. Shapiro, Marshall, and Smith 1982, p. 19.

2. Krauss 1976, p. 8.

3. Interview between the artist and Richard Marshall, quoted in Shapiro, Marshall, and Smith 1982, p. 96.

4. Correspondence with the artist, January 10, 2004, New York.

5. E-mail interview by Jock Reynolds with the artist, "Joel Shapiro: In Conversation," in Shapiro 1998, p. 25.

6. Interview with the artist in his New York studio, October 2003.

7. *Ibid.*

8. *Ibid.*

9. Shapiro 1998, p. 79.

10. Conversation with the artist in his New York studio, October 2003.

ROBERT WILSON

1. Domergue 1984, p. 167.

2. *Ibid.*

3. M. Elizabeth Osborn, "Meticulous Radiance: The Art of Robert Wilson," *Metropolis*, May 1993, p. 84.

IAN HAMILTON FINLAY

1. *Maritime Works* (Ian Hamilton Finlay and Pia Maria Simig), St. Ives: Tate St. Ives, 2002, p. 11.

ROSEMARIE TROCKEL

1. Simon 2003.

BARBARA BLOOM

1. Telephone conversation with the artist, November 20, 2003, New York.

2. *Ibid.*

DAN FLAVIN

1. Donald Judd, "In the Galleries," *Arts Magazine*, April 1964, reprinted in Judd, *Complete Writings*, 1975, p. 124.

2. Flavin was not alone in integrating electricity into his artwork. In the 1930s, Noguchi incorporated electricity in his *Lunar* sculptures; Rauschenberg used electric lights in his *Tire Lamp* and *Odalisk* in the 1950s; and both Edward Kienholtz and Jim Dine used electric lights in their reliefs in the 1960s.

3. Donald Judd, *Dan Flavin, Fluorescent Light*, Ottawa: National Gallery of Canada, October 1969, p. 199.

4. Dan Flavin quoted in *Three Installations in Fluorescent Light*, Cologne: Wallraf-Richartz-Museum and the Kunsthalle, 1973, p. 87.

5. Merleau-Ponty 1962, p. 266.

6. Baker 1988, p. 100.

7. Bruce Glaser, "New Nihilism or New Art: Interview with Stella, Judd, and Flavin," originally broadcast on WBAI-FM New York, February 1964. See Glaser 1966.

JAMES TURRELL

1. Georges Didi-Huberman, "The Fable of the Place," in Rothko, Klein, and Turrell, 2001, pp. 45–51.

2. Didi-Huberman in Rothko, Klein, and Turrell, 2001, p. 45.

3. S. Pagé, "Entretien avec James Turrell," in Turrell 1983.

4. Melinda Wortz, introduction to Turrell 1980, pp. 7–10.

5. Jan Butterfield, *The Art of Space and Light*, New York: Abbeville Press, 1993, p. 72.

6. Turrell, quoted in Dave Hickey, "James Turrell: Living in the Big Light," *Parkett Magazine* 25, 1990, p. 95.

7. Interview with the artist by Esa Laaksonen, Blaksburg, VA, 1966, http:// home.sprynet.com/ mindweb/ page44.htm, active March 2004.

8. Brooks Adams, "Three to Get Ready: James Turrell," *Art in America,* January 2000, pp. 82–87.

9. Interview with the artist by Julia Brown in Brown 1985, p. 25.

TOM SACHS

1. Julie Szabo, "The Merchandising of Tom Sachs," *Elle Decor*, October 1999, pp. 92–95.

2. Carl Skoggard, "Bitch Lounge," *nest*, Winter 1999, pp. 108–13.

3. The artist is quoted from written answers to questions posed by the author, New York, April 2004.

RACHEL WHITEREAD

1. Telephone interview with the artist, September 17, 2003. See also interview by Craig Houser, "If Walls Could Talk," in Whiteread 2001, p. 55.

2. Interview by Andrea Rose in Whiteread 1997, p. 30.

3. Houser, in Whiteread 2001, p. 53.

4. *Ibid.*

5. Jan Debbaut and Selma Klein Essink, *Rachel Whiteread,* Eindhoven: Van Abbemuseum, 1992, p. 3.

6. Rachel Whiteread, quoted in Whiteread 1997, p. 29. The full edition of ten sold immediately and has since been in production with fabrics of various colors.

7. Telephone interview with the artist, October 2003, New York.

8. *Ibid.*

JORGE PARDO

1. Christopher Knight of the *Los Angeles Times* quoted in "Jorge Pardo," *Art + Auction*, December 2003, p. 36.

FRANZ WEST

1. Franz West, quoted in Johannes Schlebruegge (ed.), *Mike Kelley, Franz West*, Vienna: P&S Wien, 2001.

2. *Ibid.* p. 37.

3. From an interview with Iwona Blazwick, James Lingwood, and Andrea Schlieker, in *Possible Worlds* 1991, pp. 83–85.

4. Franz West and Axel Huber, "3 or 17," *Parkett* 37, September 1993, p. 97.

CONCLUSION

1. Kubler 1962, pp. 1–15.

2. Conversation with the artist, October 8, 2003, New York.

Many of the quotes and ideas posited in this essay were generated in discussions with a number of the artists in the exhibition. These took place in person, via telephone, mail, and E-mail, and they constitute some of the most rewarding aspects of working on this project.

141

THEN/NOW: DECORATIVE ART BY MINIMALIST
AND POST-MINIMALIST ARTISTS AND MODERN DESIGN

JOSEPH CUNNINGHAM

The range of furniture and decorative art created by Minimalist artists in the postwar period represents some of the subtlest, and most inventive and beautiful, objects of this celebrated movement. In these works of applied art, we can see examples of the finest expressions of the minimalist aesthetic. While, as Donald Judd has pointed out, "If a person is at once making art and building furniture . . . there will be similarities,"[1] it is interesting to analyze artists' decorative objects, outside the context of painting and sculpture, against the backdrop of early twentieth-century design. In fact, formal analysis in the context of early modern design enables navigation between Judd's assertions of a near dichotomy between art and design, and the attempts of Scott Burton and Richard Tuttle, among others, to nullify that very distinction.[2]

There are clear connections between the decorative art of Minimalist and post-Minimalist artists, and masterpieces of early modern design and related vernacular forms. It is American and European early modern decorative art (c. 1880–1930), more than any other single style, that presages the design and execution of the works featured in this book. For the artists whose work appears here, the two most fundamental attractions of turn-of-the-century early Modernism are the minimalism of its aesthetic and the complexity of its subtly crafted detail (fig. 141). The seminal masterworks of the British and American Arts and Crafts, the Viennese Succession, Art Deco, De Stijl, and Bauhaus movements all influenced these artists' designs with an ascetic edge, blunted by attention to comfort and a sense of humor.

TOWARD A MINIMAL AESTHETIC: A HISTORICAL DESIGN PERSPECTIVE
Perhaps the single most important step toward a minimalist design aesthetic was taken about a century before the heyday of 1960s Minimalism by progenitors of the design-reform movement in England. In the simple and clean designs of nineteenth-century masters, from Dr. Christopher Dresser to William Morris and E.W. Godwin, the seeds of the modern aesthetic were sown (fig. 142). One of the great oddities of the history of Modernism is the extent to which the path to abstraction and a minimalist aesthetic was blazed not by painters and sculptors, but by designers of decorative art. Perhaps because of the incredible burden of throwing off the entrenched tradition of representational, illusionist painting and

142

141. Frank Lloyd Wright, *Tallback Dining-Room Chair for the Ward Willits House*, c. 1902. Quartersawn oak

142. E.W. Godwin, *Greek Chair*, c. 1883. Oak with rush seat

143. Gustav Stickley, *Bow-Arm Morris Armchair*, 1901. Quartersawn white oak

144. Pablo Picasso, *La Conversation*, 1901. Oil on cradled panel

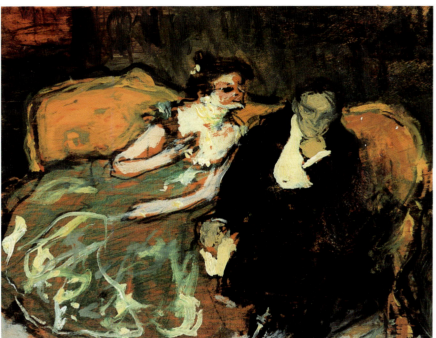

143

144

sculpture, fine art lagged significantly behind the decorative arts in embracing a thoroughgoing aesthetic of pure abstraction, and later, minimalism. In the transition from late nineteenth-century styles to the sublime simplicity of the first successes of early modern design, we can see progress toward a minimalism in the decorative arts, not achieved in the fine arts until much later (figs. 143, 144).

The English design-reform movement was the inspiration for such masters as Charles Rennie Mackintosh in Scotland, Gustav Stickley and Frank Lloyd Wright in America, and Josef Hoffmann and Koloman Moser in Vienna. These pioneers of the first decades of the twentieth century pursued a similarly straightforward, elegant domestic style, featuring an increasingly abstract geometry of form, line, and color. The beginnings of modern American design can be traced to 1893, with the chairs for Bernard Maybeck's Swedenborgian Church in San Francisco (fig. 145). This hallmark precursor of Arte Brute and Minimalism employed massive, blunt-edged wooden members, a profoundly simple composition, and a boldness of proportion worthy of the canvases of Agnes Martin or the stacked sculptures of Donald Judd.

A comparable frankness of materials (quartersawn oak), spare construction, and courage of mass distinguish the work of Gustav Stickley as among the most daring of this period. His seminal line of furniture, launched in 1901, changed the face of decorative art and introduced the beauty of simplicity into the homes and lives of thousands of Americans. Like Maybeck, Stickley rejected the fussiness and literalism characteristic of nineteenth-century styles in favor of honesty in materials and wholly unadorned surfaces. Stickley's unwillingness to indulge in his predecessors' carved and applied decorations, in the forms of flowers, animals, and landscapes, marked the first bold step toward an abstract aesthetic in American design. Likewise, in the significant achievements of Viennese designers Josef Hoffmann and Koloman Moser, we can see evidence of similarly brilliant abstraction and minimalism, all of which will help clarify formal and conceptual aspects of postwar, artist-designed minimal furniture.[3]

Frank Lloyd Wright, arguably America's most important architect, was another pioneer in the march toward abstraction, characteristic of early twentieth-century design and art. Wright's hallmark rectilinear aesthetic and boldly severe designs—introduced in decorative objects for such influential commissions as the Waller House interior (1898), the House (1900), and the Ward Willits House (1902)—are among the most subtly shaped and elegantly proportioned of any decorative art.[4] In these masterpieces, the decorated surfaces of the late nineteenth century were replaced by completely flat, simply sawn boards, in oak, pine, or plywood. Wright's emphasis on the graphic qualities of his work heightened their abstractness, and reflected both his talent as a draftsman and his desire to relate the two-dimensional format of his work to the three-dimensional—one of the defining relationships explored by the fine and decorative arts of both Donald Judd and Richard Tuttle.[5]

The subtle and elegant works of Irish designer and architect Eileen Gray stand alongside the masterpieces of these American and Viennese designers as among the most forward-looking, restrained, and ingenious works of the Modernist design canon. Bold, complex, exquisitely proportioned, Gray's hyper-modern—if not postmodern—works tested the boundaries between sculpture and decorative art. Her œuvre foretold the blurring of art and design in Scott Burton and Richard Tuttle's work, and anticipated what Tuttle has characterized as "the conversation between Minimalism and post-Minimalism" exhibited in Judd's and his works (fig. 146).[6] Another strain of Gray's decorative art demonstrates a controlled analysis of line, shape, and proportion that rivals the sculptural and design achievements of Judd and Isamu Noguchi.[7]

145

145. Bernard Maybeck and A. Page Brown, *Chair for Swedenborgian Church*, 1893. Maple

146. Eileen Gray, *Lacquered Console Table*, 1923. Lacquered wood

146

The final steps taken in the 1920s and 1930s by such design movements as Bauhaus, De Stijl, Streamline Design, and the early International School sealed once and for all the importance of the minimalist design aesthetic. The artist-designers featured in this book owe a great debt to the extraordinary men and women of these movements—from Dresser and Godwin to Gray and Anni Albers—who pioneered the minimalist aesthetic decades before steel boxes and white canvases celebrated the beauty of simplicity.

FOUNDATIONS OF ARTISTS' DESIGN: NOGUCHI'S BIOMORPHIC MINIMALISM

A discussion of the works of Judd, Burton, and Tuttle requires an exploration of the foundations laid by Isamu Noguchi in his ground-breaking abstracted designs for furniture and lighting. From the mid-1930s onward, Noguchi, who had established his reputation as a sculptor, refocused his artistic energy on creating a line of objects with which people could live and work. His pursuit of design stemmed from his exposure to the postwar art scene and the design craze of his day (especially as a designer for Herman Miller),[8] as well as to New York art society. Occasionally he experimented with shapes and textures in furniture that only appeared as motifs in his sculpture many years later. During the late 1930s and 1940s, Noguchi's seriousness as a designer of furniture nearly eclipsed his recognition as a sculptor: "As [Julien] Lévy confided after seeing Noguchi's ceramic vases: 'one sometimes wishes [Noguchi] would forego some of his more ambitious projects and give us more of these comparative trifles.'"[9] Decorative art and design were never "trifles" to Noguchi, however, who considered them a vital part of his overall approach to the integration of art and life: "It is a pity when art is to be found only in museums and in the private possessions of a few individuals. After all, culture is the integration of art and life."[10]

In his biomorphic aesthetic, Noguchi explored strange forms, odd compositions, and uncomfortable juxtapositions. In keeping with the Surrealist tendencies of Pablo Picasso in the 1930s and 1940s and the cartoon-like graphics of Arshile Gorky, Noguchi developed a vocabulary of lines, curves, and shapes that bulge, bow, and constrict, often just where you least expect. At the same time, he was exploring a similar set of minimalist design motifs, tied very closely to the biomorphic minimalism expressed in the works of his design colleagues, Charles

Eames and George Nelson, and in the works of Alvar Aalto, Frederick Kiesler, and Eva Ziesel. Noguchi's work also showed similarities with the contemporary innovations of streamline designers KEM Weber and Raymond Loewy.

In assessing Noguchi's contribution to the development of the minimalist design aesthetic, two strains of his production can be identified—the aforementioned biomorphic, represented by his *Coffee Table* (1946), and the streamline, as captured in his *Free-form Couch and Ottoman* (c. 1948; fig. 147). Understanding these objects on the basis of the biomorphic–streamline distinction reveals the particular vocabulary for each category, and interconnections across categories, clarifying the range and significance of Noguchi's design œuvre and setting up the related curvilinear and rectilinear strands of Minimalism that converse throughout the works of Judd, Burton, and Tuttle.

Noguchi's *Coffee Table*, with its bone-like, cross-stretcher base and glass top, is an icon of minimalist furniture. Its base components are closely tied to Noguchi's sculpture from the same period and have common predecessors with his *Chess Table* (1944). Carlo Bugatti's masterpiece, *Snail Chair* (1900), exhibits some of the simplified, biomorphic characteristics that later turn up as the bone-shaped stretchers on Noguchi's table.[11] The table's interlocking shapes and planes also recall the abstract Constructivism of Marianne Brandt, especially the peculiar handle of her *Teapot* of 1924, and the work of J.J. Pieter Oud, as exemplified by the counterbalance in his *Giso No. 404* (1927).[12] Finally, the glass top of the Noguchi table can be tied closely to Eileen Gray's 1935 series of *Tables*, with their dark, tubular legs and shaped wood tops, which have a very similar undulating, curvilinear articulation at their edges.

The connections between the biomorphic and streamline forms that were key to 1930s and 1940s design are manifest in Noguchi's signature *Free-form Couch and Ottoman*. In particular, the *Free-form Couch and Ottoman* are inextricably linked to the flourish of the 1930s and early 1940s designs of Frederick Kiesler and Eva Ziesel, which explored the relationship between the animism of Dada, Surrealism and early biomorphic art, and the minimal streamline design movement, of which Kiesler and Ziesel were masters.[13] Stark and minimal, Noguchi's couch and ottoman exhibit a sense of warmth and livability through their visual inseparability and the sense of humor that their whimsical shapes invoke.

147. Isamu Noguchi, *Free-form Couch and Ottoman*, c. 1948. Birch with upholstery

Almost identical in shape, design, and muted color is the Kiesler *Nesting Coffee Table* (1935–38; fig. 148). The specific kidney shape of Noguchi's couch and fitted ottoman, design details such as its small post legs, and the convex-concave fitting between the couch and the ottoman all point to the influence Kiesler probably had on Noguchi. The wave motif present in the Noguchi couch can also be linked to other important minimalist designs from the 1930s, such as Alvar Aalto's whimsically shaped *Glass Vase* of 1936, and Charles and Ray Eames's 1948 *La Chaise*—both offered in signature minimalist white.[14] With Noguchi, we can see the first steps in the tradition of artist-designed decorative arts within the context of the increasingly minimal trajectory that continues through Judd, Burton, and Tuttle.

DONALD JUDD, GUSTAV STICKLEY, AND GERRIT RIETVELD

Donald Judd's specific interest in Gustav Stickley's Craftsman furniture and related vernacular designs from the American and Viennese Arts and Crafts movements, as well as those from the Bauhaus and De Stijl movements and those by Alvar Aalto, is well documented.[15] His particular fondness for the simple Arts and Crafts aesthetic is captured in the following quotation:

148. Frederick Kiesler, *Nesting Coffee Table*, 1935–38. Cast aluminum

149. Donald Judd, installation view, *Untitled (DSS 35)*, 1963, with Gustav Stickley settle, Marfa, TX

150. Donald Judd, Mission chair with Judd wall piece, *in situ* at Marfa, TX

149

150

It's impossible to go to the store and buy a chair. In North America since the "Mission" style became unfashionable in the twenties and in England since the similar furniture derived from William Morris also became unfashionable, there has been no furniture which is pleasurable to look at, fairly available and moderate in price.[16]

Judd owned and lived with actual Craftsman examples, and, notably, many other makers' mass-produced models, leaving his several residences and commercial buildings littered with masterpieces of modern design (both antique and recent) from Stickley to Mies van der Rohe, Rietveld to Aalto (fig. 150).[17] Judd himself stated, "Mies van der Rohe is still the best and should not be considered as only a worn status symbol."[18] Peter Ballantine, a collaborator with Judd and archivist of the Judd Foundation, has suggested that, from his earliest days at Spring Street in the 1960s, Judd collected Arts and Crafts, in particular, as well as other Modernist decorative material.[19] Judd's earliest sculpture and furniture designs are blunt-edged, brutish forms, the simplicity and straightforwardness of which seem to spring from the inspiration of the vernacular Modernist designs with which he lived (fig. 149).

Judd was frequently pictured during the 1960s and 1970s standing next to, and proudly displaying, an oversized Mission chair, which he is said to have prized greatly.[20] When Judd began to think of making furniture at all, "when someone asked [him] to make a coffee table," the form of sculpture he decided to alter looked surprisingly like a Gustav Stickley Shaker-style chest.[21] It is interesting to see how Judd's sculpture was influenced also by the early Modernist design masterpieces he so loved, and, in turn, how that strain of Modernism made its way back into his design vocabulary.

Judd's specific knowledge of early modern design can be traced back to the reprinted period catalogues and other books related to the early modern American and European period that crowd his many design libraries.[22] The seminal works of Gustav Stickley and Gerrit Rietveld presage much of the Judd design vocabulary—the explorations of color, surface, and joinery, not to mention the mastery of line, shape, and proportion—on which not only his furniture but also his sculpture depend.

151

152

SETTLES AND CHAIRS

Donald Judd's attraction to the Arts and Crafts aesthetic is bound up with austerity, rectilinearity, boldness, and subtlety. Living with many Arts and Crafts settles, Judd surely recognized that the union of these features is seldom more elegant than in Stickley's *Crib* and *Knock-down Settles* (fig. 151), forms that both impress with their Modernist simplicity and aggressive boldness, and welcome with a homey casualness.[23] While the tradition of bed, couch, and daybed forms is rich and long-standing, ranging from built-in to free-standing models, Judd seems to have looked particularly at the mass, proportion, and screen-like, skirted opacity of the Stickley models in designing his *Bed #32* (fig. 153).

The enormous, unadorned slats and posts that come together to form Stickley's *Knock-down Settle* exhibit a boldness of design and elegance of proportion worthy of many of Judd's sculptures, and probably provided a model for Judd's thinking about his 1982 *Bed*. Judd creates in this bed a sense of domestic enclosure that can be compared to Stickley's *Crib Settle*. The stark simplicity of the Judd bed at first seems radically minimal, but appears more in keeping with traditions of twentieth-century Modernism when seen against the backdrop of Arts and Crafts settles that furnish many rooms throughout Judd's residences in and around Marfa. Nonetheless, Judd's manipulation of grand proportion with such minimal presence is testimony to his mastery of austere and honest structures.

The opaque pine screening created by the "floor-to-crest" sides and back of the Judd settle recalls the Prairie efforts of William Gray Purcell and George Grant Elmslie, especially in their peculiar *Armchair for the Babson House* (fig. 152). Made in 1912 for the modernizing redecoration of a 1909 Louis Sullivan house, this pioneering design introduced a skirted construction, which Judd's design so brilliantly manipulates. Judd's bed integrates restrained perpendicular angles and a seat cushion, as well as a flat-cut, exposed chair rail. While the subtly

151. Gustav Stickley, *Crib Settle, c.* 1902. Oak

152. William Gray Purcell and George Grant Elmslie, *Armchair for the Babson House*, 1912. Oak with replacement velvet upholstery

153. Donald Judd, *Bed #32*, 1982. Wood

153

proportioned members and subdued composition of Judd's bed exceed these early modern forms, they represent a tradition of austere, yet inviting, settles, on which Judd traced out his own particular vision of the form.[24]

Judd's exquisite metal *Chair #48* (1984) is one of his most outstanding adaptations of a classic early-twentieth-century form, the cube chair (fig. 154). Koloman Moser's masterpiece, the *Armchair for the Purkersdorf Sanatorium*, an undisputed Modernist highpoint, is one of the earliest expressions of the form. Designed in or around 1901 for Moser and Hoffmann's pioneering sanatorium, the armchair has been very widely shown and similar pieces remain in the collections of some of America's leading decorative-arts museums.[25] Judd is likely to have known of the chair, which he would have greatly admired. Absolutely simple in its design and execution, the armchair exhibits the rectilinear and regular-angled geometry that characterize the Judd bed. Moser's chair, like Stickley's and other mass-produced spindle cube chairs, of which Judd owned a few different models, uses the semi-opaque effect of side-slatting to create a box-like enclosure.

Offered in copper, as well as various painted-metal models, Judd's chair form exemplifies many of the most important innovations in the early development of the Minimalist aesthetic, especially the simplification of form, unity of purpose, and geometric rigor.[26] In it, we can see the effect of his corralling of energy within a smaller, more confined space, heightening density as the scale of the object is diminished. The sitter is confined immediately and completely by its metal seat, sides, and back.

The *Armchair for the Babson House* is the clearest precedent to the Judd armchair in the context of twentieth-century design history. Here, and also in the 1912 *Board-Room Armchair* for the Merchant's National Bank of Winona, Minnesota, we can see Purcell and Elmslie's fascination with creating a box-like structure in a chair form.[27] The apparently "rolled" arm-rail molding on the Winona bank armchair prefigures Judd's similar turned-metal arm treatment in his chair,

154. Donald Judd, *Chair #48*, 1984. Copper

155. Frank Lloyd Wright, *Side Chair*, 1904. Mahogany

155

and the lower terminal that completes its molded foot anticipates the rolled foot on Judd's model. In Judd's chair, the effect of rolling the arm rail downward and the foot rail upward yields unity of composition and a special density in the form.[28]

Judd's wooden slat-back chairs, the first models of which appeared in the early 1980s, and which Judd put into production around 1990, celebrate simplicity while exhibiting subtle control of complex detail. While variations in geometry below the seat relate to Judd's similar box-structure sculptures, close attention to the formal qualities of the chair designs reveals much about Judd's continued special interest in slat-back construction. As Judd was surely aware, this type of construction was a central feature of Frank Lloyd Wright's early chair designs.[29] Wright's design integrated plain geometric shapes and large slat-back panels extending uninterrupted from the crest at the top of the slat to the stretcher near the floor (fig. 155). Judd paid much heed to the success of such top-to-bottom integration of the chair form, as had Gerrit Rietveld in his celebrated *Red Blue Chair* of 1918.[30]

Judd's slat-back chairs have an antecedent in the boldly modern 1883 *Greek Chair* by E.W. Godwin, a seminal piece of early modern design. An uncompromisingly simple model, it relates closely to the simple post construction of Wright's 1904 *Slat-back Chair*. The *Greek Chair* is remarkable for its exactly perpendicular placement of the seat and rear posts, along with the creation of a box below the seat, which can be mapped on to Judd's similarly right-angled design and his inventive attention to the same boxed area under the seat. Here, Judd has invoked the slat-back tradition, while reducing the chair form to its true essence, leaving a starkly minimal assemblage of flat-cut, colored plywood boards and presenting an artistic play of geometry below the seat, which is, incidentally, useful for sitting.

TABLES AND DESKS

One of the most successful of Donald Judd's designs, his *Desk* from 1990, stems from a couple of extraordinary Gerrit Rietveld forms, which, in turn, seem to descend from Frank Lloyd Wright's early Prairie masterpieces (fig. 156). Judd, generally attracted to simpler, restrained furniture, was fascinated by the more baroque designs of Rietveld, a master of the De Stijl movement. Judd's *Desk* is a *tour-de-force* reduction of Rietveld's breathtaking Constructivist masterpiece *Sideboard*, from 1919, which exhibits the convergence of interlocking

156

157

planes and cubes, seen in both Cubism and Constructivism, not to mention the futuristic, mechanistic machinations of such artists as Francis Picabia and Marcel Duchamp, unified in a complex of micro-posts and lintels, boxes, and slat panels. At once nearly impossible to parse either formally or structurally, and yet seemingly of transparent construction, its elements appear to float by, disconnected. Similarly, Judd's *Desk* appears to speed by, revealing perhaps a time-slice of itself, rather than its true nature.

The Judd *Desk* exhibits its designer's mastery of a Minimalist, sliding-plane aesthetic through its subtle proportion, layering of presence and absence, and complex negotiation of vertical members, juxtaposed with its overriding horizontality. Judd utilizes another Rietveld innovation, the bizarre external corner-shelves exhibited in his radical 1934 *Crate Desk* (fig. 157). In Judd's reinterpretation, exposed mid-level shelves are united with the central shelf above them, forming the shelf immediately below the top surface. The lower external shelves in Rietveld's desk are joined across the expanse of Judd's desk, forming the lower shelf, as well as a kind of cross-stretcher.

The dramatic horizontality of *Desk* can also be observed in the early Prairie furniture of Frank Lloyd Wright, for instance in his *Little House Serving Table* (1902; fig. 158). Judd seems to have adapted the specific grouping of the two upper horizontals, extending the lower of the two, along with the bottom horizontal in

156. Donald Judd, *Desk #74*, 1990

157. Gerrit Rietveld, *Crate Desk*, 1934. Painted pine

158. Frank Lloyd Wright, *Little House Serving Table* designed for Francis W. Little's summer house on Lake Minnetonka, MN, 1902. White oak

159. Donald Judd, *Box Structure with Slate-top Table*, 1992

158

159

Wright's table, to the width of the table top, and emphasizing the horizontality further by reducing significantly the thickness of the boards, creating a sleek, narrow, hyper-horizontal profile. Wright himself did this in his and George Mann Niedecken's design for the *Flower Table* for the Avery Coonley House of 1908.[31] In his *Coffee Table* from the 1956 Paul Trier House, Wright again explored the possibilities of interlocking planes of exaggerated horizontal surfaces and vertical dividers, along with the exquisite innovation of the corner shelf, so brilliantly pioneered in Rietveld's table and later integrated beautifully in Judd's desk.[32]

Among the most interesting revelations when visiting Marfa is a set of slab-top and metal-frame tables that Judd made for various residences there (fig. 159). These exquisitely straightforward studies in space, line, and form both assert and deny their own presence, sometimes coming into focus against a ledge backdrop, at other times disappearing against the rustic landscape of the West Texas desert.

While their specific use by Judd is novel, cube-bottom and other open-structured slab-top tables were one of the most iconic forms of Josef Hoffmann and Koloman Moser. During the first decade of the twentieth century, Hoffmann experimented with a wide variety of simple cubic forms, as well as more complex over-arching slab examples, and a variety of oval and circular slab-topped models. His colleague Moser also created a related example in white lacquered beech in 1904. More intricate production models of these basic designs became available in the 1960s from German, Italian, American, Finnish, and other manufacturers. Especially similar to Judd's expression are the *Zelda Tables* designed by Sergio Asti and Sergio Favre for Poltronova in Italy.[33] While Judd, as an owner of pieces of Hoffmann metalwork, was probably aware of the Hoffmann examples, it may have been the later production models that provided the impetus for his reinterpretation of this compellingly sculptural, yet rustically simple, design form.

In the tradition of Godwin's *Greek Chair,* Judd's thin-post-construction tables, chairs, and stools of the late 1980s are distinctly spare in their physical presence, employing only the thinnest-possible post construction in their bold definition of the space they inhabit (fig. 160). A similar manifestation of this minimal structure can be noted in Frank Lloyd Wright's *Mori Chair* of 1915, Rietveld's 1919 *Kinderhochstuhl*, and Marcel Breuer's *Lattenstuhl* of the same year.[34] The

form of Judd's table is probably based on Rietveld's *Military Stool* of 1924 (fig. 161). This not only exhibits a similarly spare organization, but specifically expresses the simple, thin-plane top of Judd's table and stool, as well as articulating the decorative molding below it, which in Judd's brilliant interpolation becomes the elegant, if hard-to-use, undershelf.

SCOTT BURTON: ANGLE AND ARC

The rectilinear austerity and elegant proportions exhibited by the best decorative objects of Donald Judd also characterized Scott Burton's approach to furniture design. Despite his interest in blurring the distinction between fine and decorative art, Burton's keen attention to classic Modernist forms imbued his work with a range of high-Modernist motifs, from the explorations of curvilinear formalism (Bauhaus, De Stijl, Aalto) to the angular inventions of Constructivism and Art Deco. Brenda Richardson has discussed two of these influences on Burton's designs. She writes, "Burton [is] quick to credit the Constructivists as the most important artistic influence on [his] work."[35] She also notes that "The 1977 *Inlaid Table* knowingly echoes Minimalist objects in its severe geometry and galvanized steel but with equal cunning contradicts the Minimalist precedent in its use of mother-of-pearl inlays, which in furniture history recalls nothing so much as the great and ornate French designs of the eighteenth century and of Art Deco."[36] (See p. 56, fig. 48) While Richardson, along with other interpreters of Burton's work, seems adamantly protective of his creativity and originality, claiming that "sometimes Burton's objects acknowledge pioneer achievements more obliquely," she goes on to admit that, "Earlier examples in the history of art

160. Donald Judd, *Stool #68*, 1989. Cherry

161. Gerrit Rietveld, *Military Stool*, 1924. Stained plywood and elm

and design may serve Burton as specific sources of inspiration, as motives for repudiation, as the stimulus for either amicable or antagonistic dissent, or simply as the pivot for informed dialogue."[37]

In his 1983 essay, "Scott Burton Chairs," Charles Stuckey had already pointed to the important influence of the Constructivist, De Stijl, and Bauhaus movements, and especially Rietveld, on the development of Burton's creations. Stuckey quotes Burton on Rietveld:

> [Gerrit] Rietveld is not only one of the great twentieth-century furniture designers. . . . He is one of the great twentieth-century object makers, whatever that category of the object. . . . His furniture approaching sculpture (together with Brancusi's few pieces . . . that are sculpture approaching furniture) is the major precedent for any contemporary art object seeking to extend itself toward environmental and architectural design.[38]

Burton's work can be analyzed on two planes, based on his two categories of formal experimentation—the rectilinear and curvilinear. These categories are not entirely distinct, and, at his most inventive, Burton explored the peculiar interconnections of arcs and angles, and the interface that can unite curved planes with a rigorously angular structure.

ANGLE

By its very shape, Scott Burton's *Hectapod Table* (see p. 56, fig. 50), unusual among table designs of any period, immediately drives the viewer toward an understanding of it based on its perfectly regular 60-degree angles and identical, triangular top surface and side cutouts. Still, its subversion of clear sightlines provokes the viewer. Its seemingly simple geometry denies the viewer a "window on the table"— a standpoint from which to get a clear and complete view of the object.[39] In the way a Cubist painting splinters its subject, the table fractures the perception of its structure back on to the seemingly infinite number of angles from which to view it. It is precisely the straightforward geometry of the table that first encourages us to think we can grasp it—take it in at a glance—but our understanding proves fleeting and illusory, as we must embrace the complex set of relationships of angles within the table, as well as those introduced by our perspective on it.

Across early modern decorative art, there were two periods when metalwork design achieved significant advances. The origin of Modernism in metalwork is the extraordinary legacy of the early industrial designers, principal among them Dr. Christopher Dresser.[40] We see a precursor of Burton's examination of the triangular form in Dresser's *Toast Rack* of 1878, with its provocative faceting and progression of triangles.[41] The *Toast Rack* also denies the viewer a clear window, leaving the eye darting around it in search of a stable perspective. Modern metalwork's second wave of major successes came with Art Deco. Albert Cheuret's silvered-bronze and onyx mantle clock from 1925, while not strictly triangular in form, is fractured by metallic faceting into a multitude of shimmering planes. This suggests other means to think about Burton's table: its reflection of light from its surfaces, and its redirection of light back into space.

Named for an ancient architectural form, Burton's signature *Ziggurat Table* (fig. 162) of 1980 is rooted in architectural and design history. Like his *Hectapod Table,* it contorts seemingly obvious geometry. Again, we see wedge-like corner legs resulting from the negative articulation of, in this case, the ziggurat form. The square post foot—resulting from the negative expression of the base of the ziggurat shape (on each side of the table)—puns nicely on the tradition of simple, minimal feet on modern furniture designs. From this corner angle, one gets both an oblique view of the two ziggurat ascents flanking the corner proper and the revealed interior stepping of each of their solid complements. The simplicity of the object creates the effect of complex geometric perspective: "Burton's primary interest in the *Ziggurat Table* was to create a furniture form whose inside and outside were coextensive, in which the functional tabletop would be seamless in form with the table's underside."[42] This concealed-revealed aspect of the table performs a similar decentering to that of the triangular table.

Perhaps Scott Burton's most inventive furniture form is the *Slat Chair* (fig. 164). Certainly related to the investigations Burton pursued in his art, this crate-like complex, made of two triangulated forms, again demonstrates his ability to use exceedingly simple shapes to perform profound formal disruptions. The chair's structure not only distorts our understanding of its form, but also leaves us moving around the object, seeking a vantage point from which to grasp it. The specific slat construction of the chair invokes strongly Burton's peculiar

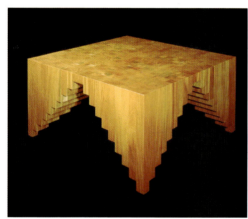

162

163

162. Scott Burton, *Ziggurat Table*, 1980

163. Carlo Bugatti, *Slatted Wood Side Chairs*, c. 1900. Wood inlaid with pewter, brass, and copper

164. Scott Burton, *Slat Chair*, 1985–86. Lacquered ash

set of historical design references—the slanted slat-back forms of both Frank Lloyd Wright and Gerrit Rietveld. Burton's specific angling of spindle planes echoes Rietveld's joining of seat and back planes in his iconic *Red Blue Chair*. The spindle construction of the planes in Burton's chair can also be traced to an even earlier precedent, an exquisite pair of Bugatti *Slatted Wood Side Chairs* from 1900 (fig. 163), which, along with Wright's use of spindles around 1899, marked the reintroduction of spindle construction in modern furniture. Bugatti's interlocking systems of parallel spindles anticipate the central intersection of Burton's design.

Interestingly, in the few years before Burton's design of the *Slat Chair*, Jim Warren produced a reinterpretation of Bugatti's great 1900 design for Pearl Dot Furniture. The interaction of spindle planes in Burton's chair suggests adjustability, but it is not, in fact, adjustable. The 1979 Pearl Dot chair amusingly folds and expands, to be used alternately as a side chair or as an elongated chaise.[43] The ideas and forms explored in Burton's interpretation of the aesthetic issues raised by these various twentieth-century design precedents show his ability to wield a complex vocabulary without sacrificing overall unity of form.

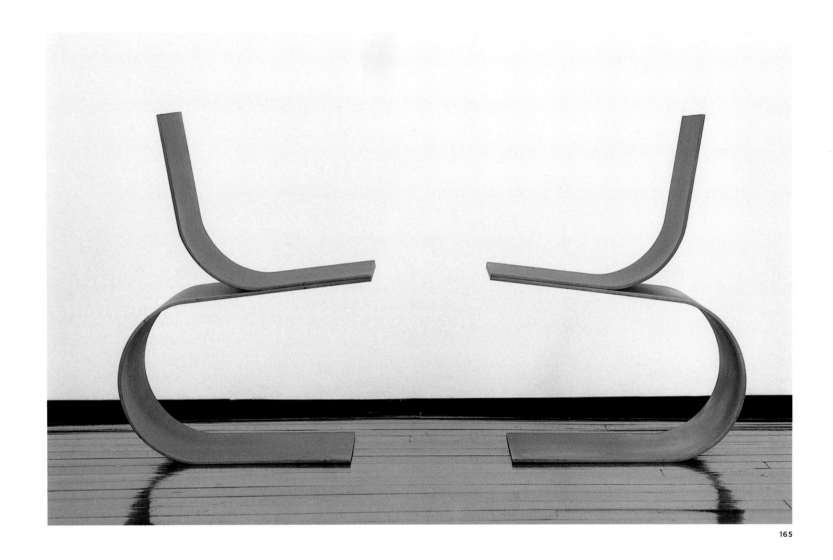

ARC

Scott Burton's *Semi-circle Table* of 1988 (see p. 59, fig. 53) celebrates a tension between the curved and the rectilinear, a theme explored from the ancients onward. The conventional desk or console shape situated above the dramatic half-round arch recalls the masterful Art Deco forms of Eileen Gray and Jean Dunand; Gray's masterpiece console table of 1923 and Dunand's eggshell-and-lacquer low tables of 1930 were the ultimate expression of minimalism in Art Deco.[44] Following these hallmark forms, Burton chose to roll the edge of the writing surface gently downward to the leg, rather than create a hard-edge angularity, such as one finds in the *Ziggurat Table*. This design signals his interest in exploring the relationship between angled and curvilinear surfaces.[45]

The antecedents of the arch itself are the work of such furniture designers as Charles Rennie Mackintosh and Harvey Ellis, with their ubiquitous arches in tables, desks, chairs, and so on, and Louis Sullivan's Prairie bank masterpieces, all around the turn of the twentieth century. In the common Sullivan motif of the half-round window within a rectilinear tiled frame, the synthesis of the two forms

165. Scott Burton, *Two Curve Chairs*, 1989. Lacquered hot-rolled steel

166. Ludwig Mies van der Rohe, *MR 10 Chair*, 1927. Chromium-plated tubular steel with woven cane

167. Gerrit Rietveld, *Zig-Zag Chair*, 1934. Painted wood

166
167

is seen with monumental effect.

The *Two Curve Chairs* that Burton made in 1989 are sublime, yet inventively subversive (fig. 165).[46] The backrest descends gently, bowing to form the seat plane, and joins gracefully to its undersupport, which in turn folds naturally, descending along an arc, eventually resting flat on the floor. This specific union of the lower curve of the chair and the substrate on which it sits was pioneered in the twentieth century by Ludwig Mies van der Rohe and used repeatedly by Alvar Aalto (fig. 166).[47] Burton's chairs can perhaps be best understood as curved reinterpretations of Rietveld's celebrated *Zig-Zag Chair* (fig. 167). Rietveld's flat backrest has been curved near the bottom, and the triangular under support for the seat has been replaced with a semi-circular one, rising from the back (as opposed to from the front support of the Mies and Aalto chairs). Both are notable feats of engineering. The intriguing shape Burton's chairs form when facing one another gives them, at once, a sculptural and an abstract appearance. Unfettered by any kind of superfluous detail that would distract from their elegant simplicity, the chairs invoke beautifully the Minimalist aesthetic, while retaining their imbalance and sense of humor.

168

THE STRANGE AND ELEGANT WORLDS OF RICHARD TUTTLE

Some of the most creative and experimental Minimalist designs have come, not surprisingly, from one of the most iconoclastic artists of the past fifty years: Richard Tuttle. The range of his output in the area of furniture, lighting, and other decorative objects is almost as wide as the incredible variety of paintings, drawings, and sculptures he has made over five decades.

Tuttle—like Judd, Burton, and Noguchi—is acutely aware of historical precedent, especially in his approach to formal issues, posed by both fine and decorative art. (See endnotes 1 and 2.) In fact, as Tuttle himself has stated, "In looking more deeply, it seems my furniture will often play with interconnecting several styles."[48] In Tuttle's mind, curious uses of shape, line, and materials recast conventional forms from chairs to chandeliers with an eye to simplicity, subtlety, and beauty. Frequently oddly shaped, his best designs exhibit elegance, while freely admitting their own uncomfortable compositions, assimilating a range of traditions—from Arts and Crafts to Art Deco to Frank Lloyd Wright—while questioning the very assumptions on which they depend. Juxtaposing unusual materials, manipulating proportion, and organizing space and line in new ways, Tuttle reforms the viewer's sensibility toward, and expectations of, decorative objects.

FURNITURE

Tuttle's subtle and elegant *Mesa Chair* (1994; fig. 168) serves as an excellent point of departure for exploring the relation of his designs to iconic forms from the early twentieth century. Its deceptively simple design employs straightforward, flat-cut poplar construction, featuring the kind of slat-back, floor-to-crest structure previously discussed. The chair is distinguished in its backrest by an unusual domed, inverted "V" crest and domed "V" reticulation, and below the seat in its similarly domed front and side cut-outs, which form the legs of the chair. The *Model No. 81 Hall Chair* of Charles Limbert (fig. 169) from almost one hundred years earlier exhibits the same level of deceptive straightforwardness, yielding upon closer examination less subtle proportion and structure in its similarly stylized piercings and its floor-to-crest, slat-back construction. In each case, the slant-angled setting of the backrest, with the seat parallel to the floor, and

169

170

171

168. Richard Tuttle, *Mesa Chair*, 1994. Poplar

169. Charles Limbert, *Model No. 81 Hall Chair*, c. 1905. Oak

170. Richard Tuttle, *Untitled (Chaise Longue)*, 1998–2000. Poplar, cotton, and polyester foam

171. Jean Dunand, *Bateau Bed*, c. 1927. Lacquered wood

the angled side panels give the chairs a sense of imbalance, almost to the point of potential disintegration on to the floor. At once perfectly at rest and teetering eerily on the edge of collapse, Tuttle's *Mesa Chair* exhibits the best of Minimalism's ability both to calm the mind and to set it in motion.

Tuttle's odd, yet successful, chaise longue (1998–2000; fig. 170) is very closely tied to the French daybeds and chaises of the Art Deco period.[49] Consisting of an opaque, molded base, invoking a boat, the chaise, despite its simple pine-board structure, has a sense of sweep, reminiscent of the masterpiece daybeds of André Arbus, Jean Dunand, Eileen Gray, and Jacques-Emile Ruhlmann (fig. 171).[50] While invoking the sweeping, boat-like form of these sleek Art Deco pieces, Tuttle's chaise puns on their very fineness, privileging his Minimalist ideals of humble materials and plain construction, while exaggerating their commonly massive size by suggesting that his design be executed in an 11-foot (3.4-m) model.[51] Perhaps attracted to their strange sense of imagery, proportion, and scale, Tuttle manipulates these oddly stylized, convoluted Art Deco designs, crossing them with vernacular beach furniture and introducing the amusing feature of adjustability. Rejecting the severity and grand elegance of the Deco forms, Tuttle replaces their pretension with uncomplicated elegance, substituting his own minimal aesthetic for their peculiar formal stylization.

172   173

Richard Tuttle's *Masculin* (2000; fig. 172) plays brilliantly, if jokingly, with the modern tradition of stacked tables, thereby resetting our expectations of the formal characteristics of tables in general. Conceptually, structurally, and functionally odd, his table at once suggests a formal openness, admitting of many uses, and yet undermines any imaginable use. The notion of a stacked table form was, curiously enough, prevalent around the turn of the twentieth century, especially in English and American furniture design. E.W. Godwin engaged with the notion of adaptability in his exceptional 1872 design for an adjustable table with folding shelves. Likewise, his 1870 occasional table featured a square-on-square structure that makes Tuttle's perversion of this sort of design so compelling.[52] The clever adjustability and regular-square stacking of Godwin's two forms may be seen to come together in the bizarre adjustability and juxtaposed square tops of Tuttle's table.

In Tuttle's *Masculin*, the through-joinery of the legs of the top table, as they pierce the lower table and descend below its surface, can be seen to have a different precedent. Frank Lloyd Wright's *Serving Table for Bradley House* (fig. 173) is exceptionally odd in its setting of a lower extended shelf (perhaps itself related to Godwin's adjustable table), with legs extended through it to support an upper shelf.[53] This highly unusual structure connects intimately with Tuttle's more disrupted construction. Inventive, strange, and ultimately moving, Tuttle's adjustable table not only provokes the viewer to reconsider what it is and how it might be used, but effects a more fundamental understanding of what tables are and why they look the way they do.

172. Richard Tuttle, *Masculin*, 2000, *in situ* in Tuttle's home. Maple plywood and plastic laminate

173. Frank Lloyd Wright, *Serving Table for Bradley House*, *c.* 1900. Oak

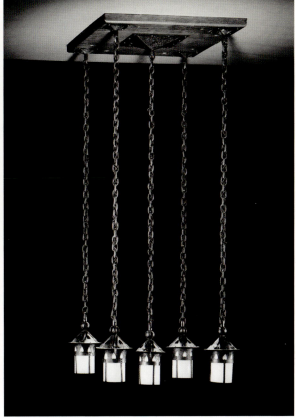

174   175

174. Richard Tuttle, *Two-light Chandelier*, 1991–98. Milk glass, iron, aluminum disc, electrical cord, and parts

175. Gustav Stickley, *Five-light Chandelier*, c. 1905. Iron and glass

LIGHTING

Richard Tuttle has also designed lighting that is every bit as imaginative as his tables and chairs. Particularly large in scope is the body of chandeliers he designed from 1991 to 1998, which continue to be produced in a small edition. Available in four prime-number configurations (2, 3, 5, and 7), the chandeliers combine simple, minimal glass-tube sleeves, reminiscent of 1960s and 1970s vernacular fixtures, with bars crafted in strange forms, typical of Tuttle's art.[54]

Tuttle's *Two-light Chandelier* (fig. 174) can be linked to Stickley's two-light chandelier (*c.* 1905), of very similar form. In each case, a wrought-iron separator solves the problem of hanging two glass lanterns in space, while ensuring they do not hit one another. In the Stickley chandelier, the separator is elegant, yet rustic; in the Tuttle piece, the metal rod functions as a drawing in space (much as Fred Sandback's yarn sculptures do). There are also similarities between Stickley's five-light and Tuttle's five-light chandeliers (fig. 175). As more lamps descend, the wrought-iron configuration becomes, in each case, more complex. In many of Stickley's chandeliers, one of two simple, cross-patterned structures is employed, while Tuttle's seizes the opportunity to add complexity to his irregular drawings in space, which hover over the lamps hanging at uneven heights below.

Was Tuttle ever able to make a *Lamp with No Style* (fig. 176)? In a sense he did, though precedents can be cited for characteristics of this work. While enigmatic to be sure, this lamp does bear a relation to Frank Lloyd Wright's inventive 1930s and 1940s furniture and to the wildly imaginative, decorative creations of Eileen Gray. Tuttle's design consists of a thin vertical, with attached mini-structures, which relate to Frank Lloyd Wright's brilliant design for a "glassless" light (*Taliesin II Floor Lamp,* 1932). Wright intentionally denies a specific point of reference in his lamp, obscuring the exact origin of each of the light sources and spinning the wooden structure around a central post that implies and denies a center, rendering impossible the location of a clear perspective. Similarly de-centered, and yet seemingly organized, the Tuttle lamp expresses our frustration in trying to make sense of the world around us and the objects in it.[55]

The origami-like construction of Frank Lloyd Wright's *Chair for Clarence Sondern House* (fig. 177) also suggests a way for thinking about the cascading, thin-board structure at the midpoint of Tuttle's *Lamp with No Style*. Tuttle articulates his admiration for this chair form and insightfully relates it to the notion of centering, when he writes: "[The chair] seems to come from two or more places without being a vortex."[56] The complex spatial relationship of these elements to the rest of Tuttle's lamp closely resembles the networks of folds, angles, and extensions he admires in Wright's inventive chairs from the 1940s and 1950s. On a lighter note, *Lamp with No Style* has a sense of animation, or even personification, which relates to the humorous invocation of animal and human forms in Memphis design.[57] While Tuttle's lamp eludes classification, it does exhibit a variety of important twentieth-century design references.

Tuttle's *Mei-Mei's Lamp* (see p. 65, fig. 59) openly puns on modern design, perhaps referring to Gerrit Rietveld's *Kinderhochstuhl* (1919). Rietveld's remarkable piece of Constructivism anticipates the precarious minimalism achieved by Tuttle in configuring *Mei-Mei's Lamp;* both structures can be best understood as a set of posts and their intersections—what could be more minimal? That does not explain the odd, simple, prefabricated shade, which descends from the top cross-post of the piece. The odd use of such simple, dangling bells as a

176

177

178   179

176. Richard Tuttle, *Lamp with No Style*, 1994. Pine, electrical parts, frosted glass, and wood screws

177. Frank Lloyd Wright, *Chair for Clarence Sondern House*, Kansas City, MO, 1939–40. Cypress with upholstery

178. Richard Tuttle, *The Smell of Trees*, 1990. Cast aluminum, ceramic, and light fixture

179. Paul Frankl, *"Skyscraper" Chair*, c. 1927–30. Lacquer and silver leaf on wood

decorative element found its earlier expression in Stickley's design for a "Two-Light Electric Lamp with . . . small shade of any plain color lined with white."[58] The Stickley model, with a brutishly simple, rustic base, demonstrates a plainness that probably informs Tuttle's own model. Although complex in its expression of Constructivist line, angle, and intersection, *Mei-Mei's Lamp* undoes its sophistication with the humorous attachment of such a mundane shade.

In *The Smell of Trees* (fig. 178), one can find, perhaps, the strangest piece of Minimalist lighting. It follows Tuttle's signature imagistic tendencies, but also evokes the aesthetic of Art Deco masters. The affinities between Tuttle's imagery and that of Eileen Gray's unusual 1920s inventions are evident in this lamp. Gray—whom Tuttle admires greatly—frequently employed strange, faceted shapes and intersecting arcs, experimenting with a wide range of unconventional materials. She, like Tuttle, felt particularly comfortable with juxtapositions of complex materials, forms, and imagery, in a wide variety of structures, yielding a body of particularly sculptural designs. Paul Frankl's exceptional *"Skyscraper" Chair* (fig. 179) design is another precedent for Tuttle's jutting, faceted boards, which capture his peculiar and creative view of the world. The metal-like surface of the faceted totems in *The Smell of Trees* relates closely to similar surfaces of Art Deco metalwork: "The surfaces of 'Smell of Trees' [are] taken from Styrofoam and plywood, surfaces to block and reflect the light, like an explosion. Surface and penetration are certainly 'modern'—which 'Trees' shatters."[59] Albert Cheuret's celebrated mantel clock and Elwood N. Cornell's pitcher and cups (1928) exploit the specific shimmer of faceted, silver objects, as they reflect and direct light, just as Tuttle's lamp creatively explores, manipulates, but also questions this effect.[60]

ANOTHER CHAPTER IN MODERN DESIGN

Rarely has more decorative art been produced by artists than in the postwar period, especially since 1980. Partly owing to the efforts of pioneering supporters of artist-designed furniture, like Elisabeth Cunnick and her New York gallery, A/D, and partly thanks to an increasing desire on the part of artists to contribute more fully to the entire domestic environments in which we live, this has been a golden age of modern design. Closely related to the proliferation of versions of Minimalism from the 1960s to the present, these works exhibit austerity and seriousness, while retaining a domestic warmth and practicality, for which they are admired by curators and loved by homemakers.

An examination of the connections between the designs of Minimalist and post-Minimalist artists and aspects of early modern design yields a number of insights into the formal characteristics of the applied arts featured in this book. It places the core of Minimalist artists' design not merely in the debt of, but, rather, along the trajectory of twentieth-century design. Donald Judd's greatest works rise to the level of those of Frank Lloyd Wright and Gerrit Rietveld; Scott Burton's innovative designs invoke comparison with Mackintosh and Bugatti; and Richard Tuttle's creative masterpieces set themselves among the achievements of Wright and Eileen Gray.

In the hands of these subtle manipulators of color, space, line, shape, and form, the Minimalist aesthetic is transformed and recast on to a spectrum of useful objects, the elegant compositions and graceful simplicity of which can inspire us every day. Not surprisingly, in creating objects for everyday use, the artists discussed here have generally employed a less-is-more sensibility, not only because of its aesthetic appeal, but also because these are, after all, objects to live with,

180. Donald Judd, installation view, *Donald Judd Furniture – Retrospective*, Museum Villa Stuck, Munich, Germany, 1993

objects to use, objects to enjoy. The same aspect of manufacture exhibited in Judd's or Burton's sculpture, for example, functions as a minimizing conceptual factor in their furniture. Richard Tuttle, on the other hand, revels in the slight differences even in manufactured goods, musing on the unrepeatability of, for example, the iron bars in his chandeliers.

The history of twentieth-century decorative art is one of the richest of any artistic period. From the late nineteenth-century rejection of applied decoration by English design reformers to the most recent work of Richard Tuttle, design has evolved through abstraction to achieve a thoroughly Minimalist aesthetic. In the best works of Minimalist and post-Minimalist design, we can see not only exploration of the beauty of simplicity, but also an innovative understanding of how we live with the objects that surround us.

1. Judd 1993, p. 7.

2. Donald Judd has asserted (notably without much argument) that "Design is not art." (Judd 1993, p. 7.) Along with many examples in the Scott Burton criticism, Richard Tuttle has distilled the opposite view of the relationship between art and design: "It is hardly necessary to distinguish between art and design." (Letter to the author, dated September 27, 2003.) For this strain of criticism on Burton, see Richardson and Waters 1986, and Mayo 1983.

3. It is worth noting that Richard Tuttle, in particular, not only admires, for example, Viennese design, but also collects it, mentioning in recent correspondence the particular connection of one of his works to a table by Otto Wagner in his collection. (Letter to the author, dated September 27, 2003.) He has even gone so far as to provide the author with a drawing of the table, along with commentary connecting it to his work *Masculin*. (Letter to the author with drawing, dated October 5, 2003.)

4. See pictures on pages 156 and 180.

5. Judd and Tuttle share a familiarity with Wright's designs. Judd's design library, still intact at the Block in Marfa, TX, is exhaustive in the area of late nineteenth-century and early twentieth-century developments. Clearly, the hundreds of books on this subject that Judd kept formed the basis for his approach not only to furniture design, but perhaps to his sculpture as well. Likewise, Tuttle has indicated an interest in, for example, Charles Rennie Mackintosh, Eileen Gray, and the International School, and collects in the area of early twentieth-century decorative arts, saying that he "tends to collect design not art." (Letters to the author, dated September 27 and October 5, 2003.)

6. See note 2, above.

7. See picture on page 163.

8. Bruce Altschuler has documented Noguchi's work with Herman Miller: "In 1944, in addition to his classic glass-topped coffee table, Noguchi designed for Herman Miller the laminated wood *Rudder Dinette Table*, its wooden fin supplemented by two bent metal legs, accompanied by companion stools of similar three-part support. . . . Available in birch, maple or ebony finish. . . ." (Noguchi 2001, p. 120.)

9. *Ibid.* p. 77.

10. Noguchi, quoted in Noguchi 2001, p. 109.

11. For illustration, see Frederick R. Brandt, *Late 19th and Early 20th Century Decorative Arts: the Sydney and Frances Lewis Collection in the Virginia Museum of Fine Arts*, Richmond, VA: Virginia Museum of Fine Arts, 1985, p. 105. Josef Hoffmann's *Table for Hermann Wittgenstein* (1905) presages the formal character of the black-lacquered base construction with shaped top of the Noguchi table. Here, the inventive cross-joined stretchers join, just as in Noguchi's table, immediately to the floor in their length, and the oval-shaped table sits upon them, as the Eames-like glass oblong does in Noguchi's expression. For illustration, see Kurt Varnedoe, *Vienna 1900*, New York: Museum of Modern Art, 1986, p. 90.

12. For illustration of Brandt's *Teapot*, see Walther Scheidig, *Crafts of the Bauhaus Weimar 1919–1925*, New York: Reinhold Publishing, 1967, p. 128; for *Giso No. 404* lamp, see *Masterworks 1900–2000*, Christie's New York, Lot 239.

13. Earlier shaped-back designs in upholstered furniture are certainly apparent in the Art Deco period, for example, in a pair of Pierre Chareau *Covered Low Chairs* (1926), which anticipate Noguchi's shaped backrest. For illustration see *Important 20th Century Decorative Arts*, Christie's New York, June 8, 2000, Lot 73.

14. For illustration of Aalto's *Glass Vase*, see Paul Johnson and Martin Eidelberg, *Design 1935–1965: What Modern Was*, New York: Harry N. Abrams, 2001, p. 96; for illustration of the Eames's *La Chaise* see Alexander von Vegesack, *100 Masterpieces from the Vitra Design Museum Collection*, Weil am Rhein: Vitra Design Museum, 1996, p. 153.

15. Donald Judd had extensive holdings of decorative art by Stickley, Wright, Hoffmann, Rietveld, Mies, Aalto, *et al.* Judd's writings include a range of commentary on twentieth-century Modernist styles and forms. See in particular, "Two Contemporary Artists Comment on Constructivism," *Art Journal*, Fall 1981, pp. 249–50; "Two Cultures," *Lotus International* 73, 1992, pp. 119–25; and "Specific Objects," *Donald Judd*, Osaka: Gallery Yamaguchi, 1992.

16. Judd, quoted in Judd 1993, pp. 8–9. He goes on to say:

> The only exception is the bentwood furniture developed by Thonet, which became less fashionable in the twenties but has continued to be made until now by Thonet and others . . . the furniture designed in the twenties by the well-known architects that continues to be made is expensive for most people and is hardly nearby to purchase. Neither is all of it agreeable. (*Ibid.* p. 9.)

17. Judd's level of connoisseurship and ability to acquire great antique objects from this period were quite limited, both because he began collecting such objects very early and because he had relatively limited means.

18. Judd, quoted in Judd 1993, p. 9.

19. Interview, September 2003.

20. Peter Ballantine and Madeleine Hoffmann of the Judd Foundation, as well as Judd's daughter, Ranier Judd, have confirmed Donald Judd's love for, and pride in, this chair. (Conversations with the author, June, July, and September 2003.)

21. Judd 1993, p. 7.

22. The range of Judd's books on early modern design is exhaustive, not to mention exhausting. Both American and European, it includes standard texts as well as a very large number of obscure, small-edition, and out-of-print examples, which would be the envy of any design and architecture researcher. These collections remain at the Block, the most substantial of his residences in Marfa, TX, and at Judd's various "miniature libraries," scattered around his other residences and commercial buildings. Judd had at his fingertips a large collection of books and periodicals relating to the entire span of architecture and design from 1880 to 1950. Peter Ballantine and Madeleine Hoffmann, as well as Rainer Judd and Marianne Stockebrand of the Chinati Foundation, Marfa, have repeatedly confirmed his knowledge of the contents of these books on early modern design. (Conversations with the author, June, July, and September 2003.)

23. Signature among the masterpieces produced by Gustav Stickley at his Craftsman Workshops are the bold, massive, and unrelentingly rectilinear settles of 1901 and 1902. During this seminal period, Stickley overthrew the excesses of late nineteenth-century design traditions, embracing a daringly austere severity never before achieved in the creation of domestic environments. For reference, see the "1902 Retail Plates," which illustrate Settle No. 173, now commonly known as the *Crib Settle*, and Settle No. 188, now commonly known as the *Knock-down Settle*; Stephen Gray (ed.), *The Early Work of Gustav Stickley*, Maplewood, NJ: Turn of the Century Editions, 1988, p. 74.

24. The flat-cut, unmolded terminus of the sides and back of the bed also recall the even-arm settles of the Stickley Brothers and other Arts and Crafts makers. The singular massiveness of Donald Judd's *Bed #32* also relates closely to Gustav Stickley's 1901 *Eastwood Chair*, a masterpiece of proto-Arte Brute, the formal qualities and enormous proportion of which may have been a model for Judd's sculpture, as well as his settle. For reference, see "1902 Retail Plates," which illustrate the *Eastwood Arm Chair*, No. 2638; *op. cit.* note 23, p. 92. The domesticity of this form is especially heightened in the brilliant, early built-in settles and inglenook surrounds of Frank Lloyd Wright, as well as in the starkly modern examples of Joseph Maria Olbrich and other Viennese designers. For reference, see illustrations of Frank Lloyd Wright's Dana House (1902) interior in Thomas A. Heinz, *Frank Lloyd Wright Interiors and Furniture*, London: Academy Editions, 1994, p. 36 (top shows built-in inglenook surround, bottom shows large, freestanding settle), and Joseph Maria Olbrich's 1905 *Inlaid and Ebonized Maple and Burrwood Upholstered Sofa* in *Important 20th Century Decorative Arts*, Christie's London, November 7, 2002, Lot 42.

25. Such museums include The Metropolitan Museum of Art and Neue Galerie, New York. For a complete history of showings of the chair, see Renée Price (ed.), *New Worlds: German and Austrian Art 1890–1940*, New York: Neue Galerie, Museum for German and Austrian Art, 2001, catalogue entry III.45, pp. 467–68; for illustration of the chair, see p. 338; and for illustration of The Metropolitan Museum of Art example, see R. Craig Miller, *Modern Design 1890–1990, in The Metropolitan Museum of Art*, New Haven, CT: Yale University Press, 1990, pp. 116–17.

26. Judd's sculpture is fabricated seamlessly and with utter precision, creating an effortless effect. Some of his furniture (especially his metal furniture, which is closest to his sculpture) expresses its joinery and construction, rather than concealing it, as is consistent with the Arts and Crafts manufacturing he so admired. In many cases, simple but elegant intersections are employed, rather than elaborately dovetailed or complex mitered joints. In the case of the metal furniture, almost all screws, nuts, bolts, and other means of connection are expressed as design elements, rather than hidden.

27. For illustration of this chair, see Jennifer Komar Olivarez, *Progressive Design in the Midwest: The Purcell-Cutts House and the Prairie School Collection at the Minneapolis Institute of Arts*, Minneapolis: University of Minnesota Press, 2000, p. 115.

28. Comparisons can also be made here to various non-rectilinear models. Josef Hoffmann's 1901–02 *Barrel Chair* creates a similar effect to that of Judd's piece, not only in the wrapped-sided, opaque contraction of the chair structure, but also in the expression of joinery-concealing pegs, placed along the seat rail, external to it. These junctures match precisely, surprisingly enough, Judd's articulation of joinery—his screw-and-nut construction on the external surface of his metal armchair. For illustration, see Varnedoe, *op. cit.* note 11, p. 85. Frank Lloyd Wright's *Mori Chair* (1915) can be linked to the Judd armchair, both in its specifically cubic manipulation of space and in its absolute simplicity. Here, a rigorous implementation of right-angle design, along with a tripartite division of space by crest rail, seat, and box-stretchers (in Judd's chair, the shelf) anticipates the matrix of structural posts in Judd's design. In particular, the *Mori Chair*'s pronounced yet subtle armrest, simple slat seat, and overall box-like structure are markedly present in Judd's later design. For illustration, see Diane Maddex, *50 Favorite Furnishings by Frank Lloyd Wright*, New York: Harry N. Abrams, 2001, p. 37.

29. As early as 1902, for the Francis Little House, Wright introduced the slat-back construction as an essential part of his chair design, a feature that can be found in his slatted chairs of 1904 for his own home.

30. For illustration of this chair, see Paul Overy, *De Stijl*, London and New York: Thames and Hudson, 1991, p. 121. Donald Judd owned a recent version of the *Red Blue Chair*, which remains installed at the Marfa Bank, in Marfa, TX.

31. For an illustration of this model, see *The Barbra Streisand Collection*, Christie's New York, November 29, 1999, Lot 494.

32. For an illustration of this model, see David A. Hanks, *Frank Lloyd Wright: Preserving an Architectural Heritage – Decorative Designs from the Domino's Pizza Collection*, New York: Dutton, 1989, p. 112.

33. For illustration of a number of international models, see *1960s Interiors and Furniture*, p. 238.

34. For illustration of the *Kinderhochstuhl*, see *Gerrit Rietveld*, Cologne: Galerie Ulrich Fiedler, 2002, p. 9; for illustration of the Breuer's Lattenstuhl, see *Important 20th Century Decorative Arts*, Christie's New York, June 8, 2002, Lot 73.

35. Richardson and Waters 1986, p. 10.

36. *Ibid.* p. 39.

37. *Ibid.*

38. Mayo 1983, p. 8.

39. This can be thought of as a visual analog of the famous argument by Richard Rorty that there are no "windows on the world," philosophically clear and clean standpoints from which to understand the world completely and objectively. As he argues in "Realism and Reference" (and again in chapter 6 of *Philosophy and the Mirror of Nature*, Princeton, NJ: Princeton University Press, 1981), the notion of *reference* as a non-intentional or "external" word–world relation that would ground our thoughts' representational bearing on things, and so explain how thoughts can so much as purport to be true, again involves illicit appeal to the idea that, independent of what we take it as, an object can have cognitive significance. An external relation of reference cannot serve as the unmoved mover of the contentfulness or aboutness of thought.

40. Dr. Dresser not only pioneered a brilliant range of profoundly forward-looking shapes and forms, he also originated the modern fascination with efficient, inexpensive ways to produce them.

41. For illustration, see *Truth Beauty Power*, New York: Historical Design, 1998, p. 37.

42. Richardson and Waters 1986, p. 39.

43. For illustration, see *Body chair*, 1979, by Jim Warren for Pearl Dot Furniture Workshops, England, in *1970s Interiors and Decorative Art*, p. 442.

44. For illustration of Dunand tables, see *Important 20th Century Decorative Arts*, Christie's New York, June 8, 2003, Lots 50 and 51. For illustration of Eileen Gray's *Lacquered Console Table*, see p. 161.

45. His specific and immediate juxtaposition of the straight-edged top surface with the elegant arch below calls to mind certain works of the Viennese designers, especially Marcel Kammerer's 1904 *Table*, by Thonet. For illustration of this table, see Varnedoe, *op. cit.* note 11, p. 89.

46. A plethora of curvilinear forms in work from Mies van der Rohe to Aalto establishes an obvious backdrop against which to understand Burton's own inquiry into the joining of arced lines and the possibilities for utterly simple forms consisting merely of these arcs and their juxtapositions.

47. For example, see Aalto's *Low Cantilevered Side Chair* of 1930–32, in *Pioneers of Avant-Garde Design*, Phillips Auctioneers, December 2000, Lot 39.

48. Letter dated October 5, 2003.

49. Tuttle says of the work's title, "'Etruscan,' comes from having made, what I consider a daybed, in Rome, finding the defeat of the Etruscans lamentable. Because it seems to have a male and female end, I wonder if it does not refer to the husband and wife reclining, funerary sculptures the Etruscans used?" (Letter to the author, dated September 27, 2003.)

50. For an illustration of a model by André Arbus, see his *Lacquered Wood and Sharkskin Gondola Bed* of 1930, in *20th Century Works of Art*, Sotheby's New York, December 6, 2002, Lot 253; for illustration of a model by Eileen Gray, see her *Canoe Sofa* from 1919–20, in *Late 19th and Early 20th Century Decorative Arts*, p. 167; for illustration of a model by Jacques-Emile Ruhlmann, see his *Upholstered Giltwood Daybed*, *Important 20th Century Decorative Arts*, Christie's New York, June 8, 2000, Lot 68.

51. This scale has never been realized, though a nearly 8-foot (2.4-m) example has been executed.

52. For illustration of these two and various related models, see Susan Weber Soros, *The Secular Furniture of E.W. Godwin*, New Haven, CT: Yale University Press, 1991, pp. 143–44, 146–47, 154–55.

53. Frank Lloyd Wright's exceptional Prairie designs first appeared in his work for the Bradley House of 1900. Here, the rectilinearity, formal simplicity, and inventive vocabulary that have become synonymous with his genius received great expression.

54. Tuttle has explicitly acknowledged the vernacular appearance of his glass cylinders and their relation to Arts and Crafts wrought iron: "I've thought how this is just a 50s cylinder lamp with wrought iron bar(s) added. Someone even said I couldn't do that! Why so insistent on wrought iron, this specific wrought iron?" (Letter to the author, dated September 27, 2003.)

55. Still, it suggests that, as Wittgenstein wrote, "the axis of reference of the examination must be rotated, but about the fixed point of our real need." (*Philosophical Investigations*, Oxford and Malden, MA: Blackwell Publishing, p. 108.)

56. Letter to the author, dated September 27, 2003.

57. Tuttle specifically referred to a Memphis vase as "good design," and admired its "very sophisticated use of style history." (Letter to the author, dated September 27, 2003.) For illustration of this Italian silver-plated vase, designed by Ettore Sottsass for Memphis, see *Important 20th Century Decorative Arts*, Christie's New York, December 8 and 9, 1995, Lot 264.

58. Tuttle has mentioned an interest in the connection between his use of antique, prefabricated "found" shades and Stickley's ordering of his bell shades, around the turn of the twentieth century. (Letter to the author, dated October 5, 2003.) For illustration, see Douglas Congdon-Martin, *The Gustav Stickley Photo Archives*, Atglen, PA: Schiffer Publishing, 2002, p. 210. Stickley's use of prefabricated glass shades was explained in an interview, March 7, 2004.

59. Letter to the author, dated September 27, 2003.

60. For an example of the Cheuret mantel clock, see *Late 19th and Early 20th Century Decorative Arts*, p. 233; for illustration of the Cornell cocktail set, see *20–21st Century Design Art*, Phillips Auctioneers, New York, May 22, 2002, Lot 34.

IT'S HARD TO FIND A GOOD LAMP

DONALD JUDD

In the middle eighties I wrote that in the middle sixties someone asked me to design a coffee table. I thought that a work of mine which was essentially a rectangular volume with the upper surface recessed could be altered. This debased the work and produced a bad table which I later threw away. The configuration and the scale of art cannot be transposed into furniture and architecture. The intent of art is different from that of the latter, which must be functional. If a chair or a building is not functional, if it appears to be only art, it is ridiculous. The art of a chair is not its resemblance to art, but is partly its reasonableness, usefulness and scale as a chair. These are proportion, which is visible reasonableness. The art in art is partly the assertion of someone's interest regardless of other considerations. A work of art exists as itself; a chair exists as a chair itself. And the idea of a chair isn't a chair. Due to the inability of art to become furniture, I didn't try again for several years. However I've always been interested in architecture and continued to sketch ideas.

Of course if a person is at once making art and building furniture and architecture there will be similarities. The various interests in form will be consistent. If you like simple forms in art you will not make complicated ones in architecture. Complicated, incidentally, is the opposite of simple, not complex, which both may be. But the difference between art and architecture is fundamental. Furniture and architecture can only be approached as such. Art cannot be imposed upon them. If their nature is seriously considered the art will occur, even art close to art itself. The mistake I made with the table was to try to make something as unusual as I thought a work of art to be. Back of this was the assumption that a good chair was only a good chair, that a chair could only be improved or changed slightly, and that nothing new could be done without a great, strange effort. But the furniture slowly became new as I dealt easily with the reality. A good chair is a good chair. The particulars slowly created the

181. Donald Judd, library at Marfa, TX

general forms that could not be directly transferred. I can now make a chair or a building that is mine without trying to derive forms from my own works of art. After a few years I designed a pair of sinks for an old building that I bought in New York City and for which I've designed much subsequently. They were designed directly as sinks; they were not a conversion; I didn't confuse them with art. The basin of the sink is an ellipse, which so far I've never used in art, instead of a circle, which I do use. I also designed a large table with chairs, some-what like benches, to be made of folded $\frac{1}{8}$-inch stainless steel, brass or copper. This was never made because the fourth floor of the building in which it was to be is very open, primarily two planes, floor and ceiling, while the table and chairs are very closed. The latter would ruin the space. I later made some bookshelves for the third floor.

I kept the building but moved to West Texas with my two children, where I rented a small house on the edge of town. The house was quartered into eleven-by-eleven-foot rooms. There was no furniture and none to be bought, either old, since the town had not shrunk or changed much since its beginning in 1883, or new, since the few stores sold only fake antiques or tubular kitchen furniture with plastic surfaces printed with inane geometric patterns or flowers. The two small children played and slept in one of the four rooms. In order to give them each an area of their own notwithstanding the one room, I designed a bed which was a closed platform of one-by-twelves with a central, free-standing wall, also of one-by-twelves. The bed was designed so that the lumber yard could cut the different lengths to size and I could then nail them together in place. I liked the bed a great deal, and in fact the whole house, for which I made other furniture. Later, in a large place in town, I designed desks and chairs for the children using the same method of construction. More furni-ture developed from this beginning.

It's impossible to go to the store and buy a chair. In North America since the "Mission" style became unfashionable in the twenties and in England since the similar furniture derived from William Morris also became unfashionable, there has been no furniture which is pleasurable to look at, fairly available and moderate in price. The only exception is the bentwood furniture developed by Thonet, which became less fashionable in the twenties but has continued to be made until now by Thonet and others. This is still not expensive but it is not down the street in the store. The furniture designed in the twenties by the well-known architects that continues to be made is expensive for most people, although not as expensive as the materials and the construction imply, and is hardly nearby to purchase. Neither is it all agreeable. Mies van der Rohe's is still the best and should not be considered as only a worn status symbol. As bad ideas should not be accepted because they are fashionable, good ideas should not be rejected because they are unfashionable. Conventions are not worth reacting to one way or another. Most of the other furniture in production, such as Breuer's Wassily chair and Le Corbusier's furniture, is an early civilized and almost forgivable sentimentalizing of the machine. The chairs of both architects are derived from the better camping and military chairs of the nineteenth century. Old good ideas made new and shiny are now a dismaying precedent. Sentimentalizing the machine is now a malignity of the century. This is present in most available furniture and in most buildings. It is extreme in Pompidou and Lloyd's. In furniture this puerility is usually combined with the puerility of domesticity, the societal progress of the machine with personal progress in the society.

Almost all furniture made since the twenties and much before in any of the styles, "modern" and "traditional," has been junk for consumers. As I've written, the ornate and overstuffed furniture of the last half of the nineteenth century, crowded into corresponding rooms, was not supplanted by simple and functional modern furniture. Instead, this was turned into Victorian furniture, also crowded into matching rooms. Decoration isn't just applied; a chair is decoration. Modern, progressive furniture has been corrupted into the opposite. Primarily, "traditional" furniture, Victorian furniture, continues. It's ordinarily what's in the store. This is what most people have to choose from, whether in Yellowknife or New York. As in politics, this furniture is not traditional and conservative but is an imitation of past furniture. The appearance of the past represents status by invoking a higher class in the past than the purchaser is in the present. The imitation old furniture symbolizes up and the imitation modern symbolizes forward. Usually the first is in the home and the second is in the office, sometimes one or the other in both, and seldom the reverse. Good office furniture is also difficult to find. The bizarre and complicated "modern" office of the rich executive, who has photographs on his desk of his wife and children in their traditional setting, is a summation of the surrounding corporate headquarters. Since he or his wife is on the board of the museum, it must look progressive, like the headquarters, but with a touch of tradition, for her, for upward mobility to the past, for something better than business, such as learning, although there is nothing better, and generally for the gentility of art, which symbolized all of these. Then, also, he may be on the town council, or he builds shopping centers, or he builds apartment houses, giving the people what they want, to go with the furniture in which they had no choice. Upward and forward, and lower every year, not only in architecture and art, but economically and politically, since reality is equally absent. Anyway, what kind of a society is it when you can't even buy a chair?

Architects, designers, business people, even politicians say that they are giving people what they want. They are giving the people what they deserve, because of their negligence, but they are presumptuous to claim to know what they want. What they want is what they get. An exception to imposing upon the public what they want, or perhaps a rare good guess, is the design of Sony television sets and other equipment, of some other Japanese companies and of some European companies. This has no relation to traditional Japanese architecture, which is fortunate, because if it did the new version of the old would be just as debased as it is in the United States. Department stores in Osaka are floor after floor kitsch, as they are in New York. And always surprisingly, and always, everywhere, new Japanese architecture, and Korean, show no fundamental lessons learned from their past architecture, the same as in Paris. In the United States the television machine began disguised and continues as at once the myth of the machine and the myth of the old home. The Americans gave the Americans what they wanted; they didn't want it. Neither did anyone else. In addition to the success of Sony's design, there is the smaller success of Braun, whose design must be the model, somewhat better as earlier usually is, for Sony's design. A few months ago there was a curious article in Lufthansa's magazine justly praising Braun and its chief designer, Dieter Rams, praising "German" design of course, but explaining that "German" design was now second to "Italian" design (consumer products are not where nations differ in design) but that Germany would catch up. This means become worse. "Designer" Italian furniture is the world's worst. The only things as bad are the plastic bottles for liquid soap. It is an exception and a possibility that you can go down the street and choose a TV and enjoy looking at it when it's turned off. In Texas, when I made the first furniture, I wanted a television set. This wasn't down the street, but almost twenty-five miles away. All the sets were American, all were made of plastic imitating wood, some like your Anglo grandmother's sideboard, some like your Italian grandmother's *credenza*, some like your Latino grandmother's *aparador*. I chose an Anglo set by Zenith. Again as usual, the design and the technology were congruent. The color was that of the first colored comic strip, printed during an earthquake.

Most of the furniture that I have designed remains fairly expensive, because of its methods of construction, and it is not easily available. We have made a serious effort to lower the prices but the furniture is handmade, basically even the sheet-metal pieces made by Janssen, one by one. These would be cheaper made by hundreds but still there would be considerable handiwork. The wooden furniture cannot change. Lower prices require great numbers which require a large distribution. This usually leads to the department store. The distribution of furniture, and of books, probably of most things, are monopolies against diversity, which eliminate exceptions and complications, which have an invariable scheme for production and for costs, and of course for appearance, and for books, subject-matter. For both furniture and books the designer and the author receive absolutely very little. The production cost of furniture is not as fixed as the cost of the designer, but it is low. The cost of the designer must have developed from that of real modern furniture, since the architect was always dead. The producer, not the factory, and the retailer, or both as one, receive the most money, some as profit, some for the expenses of the distribution and the salesroom. This makes an impossible price. And of course it seems that the middleman should get less. The larger the distribution the more to the middleman. Therefore the best method is a small distribution, which is what we do. And, importantly, we are the producers, which combines that profit and my profit into one, leaving only the retailer as extra. Our furniture goes around the world, but only one by one. Most things could be made in the area in which they are consumed, eliminating the big distributor, often one company charging for three functions, instead of two for one as in our case, charging three times as the distributor, the producer and the manufacturer, that is, profiting as corporations. Almost anything they can do anyone can do anywhere. And obviously even cars and TVs could be made by any large city or small country. I have always thought it strange that there are no cars made in Switzerland. I have heard that there once was a company. Why should Texas import cars and trucks from Michigan? The oligarchy of monopolies of distribution prevents innovations, invents only restrictions, and raises blank walls. The flat and boring society is a maze of blank walls just above eye level. This prevents new and real inventions, so obviously there is no chance for only a new chair or a little book. The purpose of big business is to maintain its oligarchy rather than to do anything else, for example, to fulfill its two biggest claims, competition and innovation. Efficiency is another claim, part of progress, efficiency for profit, not necessarily for production, and not for the public. Only in the mythical "progress" is there a suggestion of benefiting society. Most business people think that such slight altruism is part of their advertising. And "free enterprise" is a slogan of the Pentagon.

Noam Chomsky writes:

> Free trade is fine for economics departments and newspaper editorials, but nobody in the corporate world or the government takes the doctrines seriously. The parts of the U.S. economy that are able to compete internationally are primarily the state-subsidized ones, capital-intensive agriculture (agribusiness, as it's called), high-tech industry, pharmaceuticals, biotechnology, etc.

The same is true of other industrial societies. The U.S. government has the public pay for research and development and provides, largely through the military, a state-guaranteed market for waste production. If something is marketable, the private sector takes it over. That system of public subsidy and private profit is what is called free enterprise.

My experience is that both furniture distribution and book distribution are impossible. On the other hand the art business is such a one-horse business that something larger seems better. But this is perhaps because the context for art is so weak. The only possible way perhaps to make cheap mass-produced furniture is to start with a construction cost and to design accordingly. At present we would have to debase the construction of the existing furniture for mass production. Beginning from a fixed construction cost still leaves the questions of too little to the designer and too much to the producer–organizer–wholesaler and to the retailer.

The roughly made pine furniture made by me and others in Texas was made first, with a few exceptions. So far this has not been made for sale. Next, well-made furniture in fine solid wood was made for my building in New York and then in small numbers to sell, as it still is. The wood and the craftsmanship make this the most expensive. In '84 I designed some chairs, benches, a table and some beds in sheet metal, which were painted one color to a piece. There were also a couple of chairs and a table made of copper. This was for myself but also was the first furniture to begin as furniture to sell. Since this was sheet metal and the construction was common, I thought it would be cheap enough to be used outdoors in public, but there is still too much handiwork. Until then, except for the first pine chairs, all of the furniture was somewhat heavy. Five years ago I designed some light chairs and two tables in solid wood. These are simply but well made in Yorkshire. Similar ones were made recently for outdoors in galvanized steel and of granite, again heavy, and also in Texas in painted steel and of slate. A few years ago, first for use, then for sale, desks, tables and a bench were made in Cologne of clear plywood. The sheets of plywood are cut as little as possible and are slipped together, interlocking, like a children's toy, an old idea. These also, sometimes with the plywood coated commercially with a color, as well as chairs like those in pine, are made in New York.

I am often asked if the furniture is art, since almost ten years ago some artists made art that was also furniture. The furniture is furniture and is only art in that architecture, ceramics, textiles and many things are art. We try to keep the furniture out of art galleries to avoid this confusion, which is far from my thinking. And also to avoid the consequent inflation of the price. I am often told that the furniture is not comfortable, and in that not functional. The source of the questions is in the overstuffed bourgeois Victorian furniture, which as I said, never ceased. The furniture is comfortable to me. Rather than making a chair to sleep in or a machine to live in, it is better to make a bed. A straight chair is best for eating or writing. The third position is standing.

© 1993 Donald Judd

EXCERPT: SITUATION ESTHETICS
SCOTT BURTON

The very idea of audience is reappearing. It isn't just a question of the nature of an audience—what class or caste is reflected—but of the nature of the work's relationship to audience. A new kind of relationship seems to be beginning to evolve, a deep shift beginning in our needs toward a visual culture of design or applied art. The new descriptive phrases for this culture haven't been coined yet, but it might be called public art. Not because it is necessarily located in public places, but because its content is more than the private history of its maker. It might be called popular art, not because it is a mass art, but because it is not an unpopular art, not a "difficult" or "critical" art. Visual art is moving away from the hermetic, the hieratic, the self-directed, toward more civic, outer-directed, less self-important relations with social history. No mere maker of visual signs can be exemplary, can propose a sufficient moral authority or model of psychic liberation in a time like ours, a time convinced that it is proceeding toward apocalypse. Art just seems spiritually insufficient in a doomsday climate and it will take an increasingly relative position. It will place itself not in front of but around, behind, underneath (literally) the audience—in an *operational* capacity. This doesn't mean that monumental forms will die out. On the contrary.

I see at this time two main mutations of art. They come out of sculpture and painting but leave them behind. One is a new architecturality—I mean the landscape architecture of George Trakas and the interior architecture of Siah Armajani. These artists have advanced beyond architecture sculpture to the category of actual buildings, for the structures of Trakas and Armajani are not to be experienced for their own sakes. Instead, they shape or enhance—they operate on—the user's experience (respectively, of the landscape itself and the social function). The audience's use of these artists' structures is their very meaning. The counterpart of the new building art is the new decorative art. Its makers have emerged from painting and will eventually renew craft, they do not use

182. Scott Burton, *Atrium Furbishment*, 1984-86. *Verde Larissa* marble semi-circular setee with pink onyx lights and circular table

decorativeness as a realm of pictures but are rediscovering other categories of artifact—furnishings and architectural decoration found in the lamps of Harry Anderson, the screens, curtains and hangings of Robert Kushner, Jane Kaufman and Kim McConnell, the walls, floors and ceilings of Joyce Kozloff and Valerie Jaudon. Professional designers and craftspeople don't have the powers of invention that these and a few other artists are being given by the historical moment.

Somewhere between these two new forms I locate my own objects, my furniture. And there is an important related artist who has appeared at this time, too—Judith Shea, the clearest, most advanced artist who produces wearable objects. Her work is clothing, not costume, she is rethinking the structure of Western garments, much as Steve Reich rethought the structure of our music, and in a way only an artist, as opposed to a fashion designer, has today the cultural freedom to do (for the art world still has its uses).

My own history in performance leads me to add the point that there is a parallel mutation toward audience-oriented work in this field. The pioneer of the emergent entertainment performance as opposed to the self-investigation of "conceptual performance," is Alan Suicide. From the beginning, this music-artist took performance to real stages, to clubs and cabarets, and in the process was an innovator of contemporary personal style (Punk). Related is William Wegman, who introduced a classic means of audience accessibility, humor, into art, thus moving the visual culture away from video art and toward television.

All this will take several generations; it's not just a matter of new styles which can appear and disappear within a decade. There are still painters and sculptors whose talents are large enough to give their art forms some historical vitality— though there are fewer and fewer.

Artforum, January 1980

THESIS, ANTITHESIS, SYNTHESIS
RICHARD TUTTLE

Although artists have made furniture before, this recent involvement is unparalleled, I would say, for a number of reasons. An exhibition like *Design ≠ Art* reveals enough material to make our judgment about that statement, resting as it does in the great Cooper-Hewitt tradition of quantitative assessment. It is a unique window to our times if the material is structured properly for our mind's enjoyment. The structure I am proposing would use the time-honored, three-part structure of thesis, antithesis, and synthesis to apply to Donald Judd, Scott Burton, and me, in that order.

Judd has superlative qualities as thesis-maker: rigor, fearless position-taking, confidence in himself—personal qualities, but he also has a position with the weight of history behind it. Strong in everyway, he plants a wedge between sculpture and furniture design. Erstwhile Scott Burton appears next, questioning the conservatism of the thesis. Perhaps he doesn't understand the revolutionary radical, and thinks it can be re-housed by joining sculpture and furniture design? He writes about this: a sculpture is a chair. The illusion in his design is always corrected by being a bench, table, *etc.*, manifestations of sculpture. Like Judd's, it is a classicist position, but he is careful to insist the works are sculptural, bringing in humor and making them Public Art in many cases, accessible, if cold, in the end.

The problem, then, is to satisfy sculpture and furniture design in one work. Using the great Scots architect Charles Rennie Mackintosh as inspiration, his special ability to create new forms by synthesizing, bringing two things together, the horizontal and the vertical, the old and the new, you have works like my *The Nature of the Gun*, *Mei-Mei's Lamp*, and *Masculin*. Cube-based, all this work fuses elements of the polarities hidden within art and design—could not have been made without them—and sustains the thesis of Judd and accommodates the antithesis of Burton.

What is remarkable in this seemingly linear breakdown, played out as it is against the 1970s, 1980s, and 1990s, is that each of these positions, in my opinion, was formed at precisely the same time!

183. Richard Tuttle, *Untitled (Chaise Longue)*, 1998–2000. Poplar, cotton, and polyester foam

TIMELINE

ELIZABETH CHASE

1904	Isamu Noguchi born in Los Angeles	**1951**	Noguchi designs a garden for the Tokyo offices of *Reader's Digest*, and first *Akari* lamps, including the *#33N*
1924	Richard Artschwager born in Washington, D.C.		
1925	Ian Hamilton Finlay born in Nassau, Bahamas		Barbara Bloom born in Los Angeles
	Robert Rauschenberg born in Port Arthur, TX	**1953**	Rosemarie Trockel born in Schwerte, Germany
	Russian Constructivist Aleksandr Rodchenko's experimental environment called the *Workers' Club* shown at the *Exposition Internationale des Arts Décoratifs et Industriels Modernes*	**1956**	Chamberlain exhibits his art at the Martha Jackson Gallery, New York
		1957	Artschwager participates in a show of furniture by craftsmen at the New York Museum of Contemporary Crafts
1927	Noguchi serves as studio assistant to Constantin Brancusi in Paris		Noguchi designs *Alcoa Forecast Program Tables*
	John Chamberlain born in Rochester, IN	**1958**	Rauschenberg mounts his first solo exhibition, which includes combines, at the Leo Castelli Gallery, New York
1928	Donald Judd born in Excelsior Springs, MO		
	Sol LeWitt born in Hartford, CT	**1960**	Chamberlain's first major solo show of scrap-metal sculptures opens at the Martha Jackson Gallery, New York
1933	Dan Flavin born in Jamaica, NY		
1937	Noguchi's *Radio Nurse*, a nursery intercom, commissioned by Zenith	**1963**	Jorge Pardo born in Havana, Cuba
			Rachel Whiteread born in London, England
1939	Noguchi designs *Goodyear Table* for A. Conger Goodyear	**1964**	Flavin mounts a solo exhibition of his first light sculptures, *icons*, at the Kaymar Gallery, New York
	Scott Burton born in Greensboro, AL		
1941	Joel Shapiro born in New York	**1965**	LeWitt makes his first table
	Richard Tuttle born in Rahway, NJ		Tom Sachs born in New York
	Robert Wilson born in Waco, TX	**1966**	*Primary Structures* exhibition, including works by Artschwager, Judd, Flavin, and LeWitt, opens at The Jewish Museum, New York
1943	James Turrell born in Los Angeles		
1943–44	Noguchi designs the three-legged cylinder lamp	**1967–71**	Chamberlain designs *Judd Couch*
1947	Franz West born in Vienna, Austria	**1968**	Wilson founds Byrd Hoffman School of Byrds in a loft on Spring Street, New York
	Bryan Hunt born in Terre Haute, IN		
1949	Artschwager arrives in New York as an artist and starts making furniture to earn a living		Judd retrospective opens at the Whitney Museum of American Art, New York
			Judd buys 101 Spring Street, New York

| 1969 | Pardo moves to the United States |
| | Wilson designs *Light Bulb* for his production of *Death, Destruction, and Detroit* |

1969	Pardo moves to the United States
	Wilson designs his first chair, for the play *The Life and Times of Sigmund Freud*
	Flavin retrospective opens at the National Gallery of Canada, Ottawa, and The Jewish Museum, New York
Late 1960s	Shapiro emerges as one of the New York avant-garde artists known as post-Minimalists, as do Benglis, Hess, Le Va, Nauman, Serra, Smithson, and Tuttle
1970	Shapiro's first exhibition opens at the Paula Cooper Gallery, New York
	Judd begins designing furniture
1970–71	Judd designs *Spring Street Sink and Shelf*
1971	Rauschenberg designs *Tire Lamp*
1971–72	Chamberlain retrospective at the Solomon R. Guggenheim Museum, New York
1971–80	Burton's *Behavior Tableaux* is performed at the Whitney Museum of American Art, New York, the Solomon R. Guggenheim Museum, New York, and other museums
1972	Burton designs first chair, *Bronze Chair*
	Judd moves to Marfa, TX, part-time
	Tuttle mounts *Projects: Richard Tuttle* at the Museum of Modern Art (MoMA), New York
1973	Hunt makes his first table
1974	Turrell works on his first large *Skyscape*. He also relocates to Roden Crater, AZ, where he continues to work today
Mid-1970s	West starts producing *Adaptives*
1976–79	Burton designs *Lawn Chairs (a Pair)*
1977	Judd designs prototype for *Child's Desk*
	Hunt makes first steel and glass table
1978	Burton designs *Child's Table and Chair*
1979	Chamberlain designs the Federal Plaza in Detroit

	Wilson designs *Light Bulb* for his production of *Death, Destruction, and Detroit*
1980	Shapiro starts installing sculptures in outdoor public spaces
	Burton designs *Rock Chairs (A Pair)*
	Turrell retrospective opens at the Whitney Museum of American Art, New York
1981	LeWitt designs *Coffee Table*
	Bloom's *The Village People* installation at *Westkunst-Heute* exhibition, Cologne, Germany
1982	Burton designs *Hectapod Table*
	Shapiro solo exhibition at the Whitney Museum of American Art, New York
1983	Judd designs *Bookcase #34*
1984	Judd designs *Wintergarden Bench #16/17, Yellow Stool #43, Metal Chair #46*, and *Chair #48*
1985	Trockel starts series of knitted works
	Burton designs *Low Piece*
	Hunt designs *Library Table*
1986	LeWitt designs *Folding Screens*
	Trockel designs striped carpet, *etc.*, for the German embassy in Washington, D.C.
1987	Trockel designs *Plus-Minus* rug
	Wilson designs *Parzival: a Chair with a Shadow*
	Judd designs *Bed #32*, and *Chairs #84/85 (two of a set of ten variations)*
1987–90	Artschwager designs *Chair/Chair*
1988	Noguchi dies in New York
	Burton designs *Semi-circle Table*
	Whiteread's first gallery exhibition, at the Carlisle Gallery, London. The show features furniture, such as wardrobes, bathtubs, and mattresses, cast in plaster
	Bloom's *Esprit de l'Escalier* wins the Due Mille Prize, *Aperto*, Venice Biennale

1989	Wilson designs *Pierre Curie Chair* (for the play *De Materie*)	**1996**	Flavin dies in Riverhead, NY
	Burton designs *Two Curve Chairs*		Chamberlain designs *Tasted Snow* dinnerware set
	Burton dies in New York		Shapiro makes plaster prototype table
	Artschwager designs *Klock*	**1997**	Tuttle designs *"Is there a . . .?"* carpet
	Tuttle designs *Mei-Mei's Lamp*	**1998**	Turrell designs *Lapsed Quaker Ware*
	Bloom's *The Reign of Narcissism* is exhibited at the Los Angeles Museum of Contemporary Art		West designs *Creativity: Furniture Reversal* chairs, table, and lamp
	Judd designs *Stool and Table #68*, *Chair and Armchair*, and *Two Corner Chairs #72*		Rauschenberg retrospective opens at the Solomon R. Guggenheim Museum, New York
Early 1990s	Turrell starts designing functional objects	**1998–**	Wilson designs *Angel Glassware* (set of glasses with wing variations)
1990	Tuttle designs *The Smell of Trees* lamp and *The Nature of the Gun* suite of furniture	**1999**	Bloom designs *Lolita* rug
	Trockel designs *The Painting Machine*		Whiteread mounts her first major furniture exhibition; designs *Daybed*
	Judd designs *Desk #74* and porcelain table service		Sachs designs *Bitch Lounge*
	Flavin designs *For André Raynaud* porcelain plates	**2000**	Tuttle designs *Masculin* table
1991	LeWitt designs *Metal Coffee Table*	**2001**	Finlay designs *Sails/Waves* blanket
	Judd designs *Bed #87*		Bloom's *Broken* exhibition at Gorney, Bravin + Lee, New York
1991–98	Tuttle designs *Cylinder Chandeliers*		*Joel Shapiro on the Roof* exhibition at The Metropolitan Museum of Art, New York
1992	West's *Auditorium* installation is completed at Domaine de Kerguéhennec, Bignan, France	**2002**	LeWitt designs *Untitled: Set of 4 Crystal Glasses*
	Donald Judd designs *Desk with Two Chairs #97*	**2003**	Tuttle designs *Turbulence Chair*
	LeWitt designs *High Table*		Pardo designs *Untitled (Floor Lamps)*
1993	Judd designs prototype for *Pine Table*		Shapiro designs *Giraffe 2003*
1994	Tuttle designs *Lamp with No Style*	**2003–04**	Shapiro designs 'untitled' (plaster prototype)
	Tuttle designs *Mesa Chair* and maquette of *Cylinder Chandelier*	**2004**	Hunt designs *Island Table*
	Shapiro designs 'untitled' (bronze table)		
	Whiteread wins Turner Prize		
	Judd dies in New York		
1994–98	Pardo designs 4166 Sea View Lane for a project with the Los Angeles Museum of Contemporary Art		

SELECTED REFERENCES

Adams, Brooks. "Three to Get Ready: James Turrell," *Art in America* 88, no. 1 (January 2000), pp. 82–87

Alexander, Brooke. *Richard Artschwager: Complete Multiples.* New York: Brooke Alexander Editions, 1991

Altshuler, Bruce. *Isamu Noguchi.* New York: Abbeville Press, 1994

Antonelli, Paola, *et al. Sitting on the Edge: Modernist Design from the Collection of Michael and Gabrielle Boyd.* San Francisco: San Francisco Museum of Modern Art and Rizzoli International Publications, New York, 1998

Apostolos-Cappadona, Diane, and Bruce Altshuler (eds.). *Isamu Noguchi: Essays and Conversations.* New York: Isamu Noguchi Foundation and Harry N. Abrams, New York, 1994

Armstrong, Richard. *Richard Artschwager.* New York: Whitney Museum of American Art, 1988

Artschwager, Richard. *Richard Artschwager.* Ithaca, NY: Herbert F. Johnson Museum of Art, Cornell University, 1998

Artschwager, Richard, and Michael Lobel. *Richard Artschwager.* London: Gagosian Gallery, 2003

Auping, Michael. *John Chamberlain: Reliefs, 1960–1982.* Sarasota, FL: John and Mable Ringling Museum of Art, 1982

Baker, Kenneth. *Minimalism: Art of Circumstance.* New York: Abbeville Press, 1988

Battcock, Gregory (ed.). *Minimal Art: A Critical Anthology.* New York: Dutton, 1968

Benjamin, Roger. *Matisse's "Notes of a Painter": Criticism, Theory, and Context, 1891–1908.* Ann Arbor, MI: UMI Research Press, 1987

Bloem, Marja (ed.). *John Chamberlain: Current Work and Fond Memories; Sculptures and Photographs, 1967–1995.* Amsterdam: Stedelijk Museum, 1996

Brown, Julia. *Occluded Front: James Turrell.* Los Angeles: Museum of Contemporary Art and The Lapis Press, Larkspur Landing, CA, 1985

Burton, Scott. "Furniture Journal: Rietveld," *Art in America* 68 (November 1980), pp. 102–108

Chamberlain, John, and Pace Wildenstein Gallery. *John Chamberlain: Recent Work.* New York: Pace Wildenstein Gallery, 1992

Chamberlain, John, and Pace Wildenstein Gallery. *John Chamberlain: Recent Sculpture.* New York: Pace Wildenstein Gallery, 1994

Chamberlain, John, and Diane Waldman. *John Chamberlain: A Retrospective Exhibition.* New York: Solomon R. Guggenheim Museum, 1971

Cooke, Lynne. *Scott Burton: Early Work.* New York: Max Protetch Gallery, 1990

Domergue, Denise. *Artists Design Furniture.* New York: Harry N. Abrams, 1984

Duchamp, Marcel. *Salt Seller: The Writings of Marcel Duchamp.* Edited by Michel Sanouillet and Elmer Peterson. Oxford and New York: Oxford University Press, 1973

Elgar, Dietmar (ed.). *Donald Judd: Colorist.* Bonn: Hatje Cantz Verlag, 2000

Farr, Christopher, Matthew Bourne, and Fiona Leslie. *Contemporary Rugs: Art and Design.* London: Merrell Publishers, 2002

Forge, Andrew. *Rauschenberg.* New York: Harry N. Abrams, 1969

Gallagher, Ann (ed.). *Rachel Whiteread,* British Pavilion, 47th Venice Biennale exhibition catalogue, London: British Arts Council, 1997

Garrels, Gary (ed.). *Sol LeWitt: A Retrospective.* New Haven, CT: Yale University Press, 2000

Glaser, Bruce. "New Nihilism or New Art: Interview with Stella, Judd, and Flavin," original broadcast WBAI-FM New York, February 1964. Reprinted in *Art News* 65, no. 5 (September 1966), pp. 55–61

Graham, John. *System and Dialectics of Art.* Edited by Marcia Epstein Allentuck. Baltimore: Johns Hopkins University Press, 1971

Gray, Camilla. *The Great Experiment: Russian Art, 1863–1922*. New York: Harry N. Abrams, 1962

Greenberg, Clement. "Recentness of Sculpture," *American Sculpture of the Sixties*. Edited by Maurice Tuchman. Los Angeles: Los Angeles County Museum of Art, 1967

Haskell, Barbara. *Donald Judd*. New York: Whitney Museum of Art and W.W. Norton & Company, New York, 1988

Hunter, Sam. *Robert Rauschenberg*. New York: Rizzoli International Publications, 1999

Judd, Donald. *Complete Writings 1959–1975*. New York: New York University Press, 1975

Judd, Donald. *Donald Judd: A Catalogue of the Exhibition at the National Gallery of Canada, Ottawa, 24 May – 6 July, 1975; Catalogue Raisonné of Paintings, Objects, and Wood-Blocks, 1960–1974*. Ottawa: National Gallery of Canada, 1975

Judd, Donald. *Donald Judd Furniture Retrospective*, Rotterdam: Museum Boymans–van Beuningen, 1993

Kelly, Ellsworth, and Gottfried Boehm. *Ellsworth Kelly: Yellow Curve*. Stuttgart: Edition Cantz, 1992

Kelly, Ellsworth, *et al. Ellsworth Kelly: Red, Green, Blue; Paintings and Studies, 1958–1965*. La Jolla, CA: Museum of Contemporary Art San Diego, 2002

Krauss, Rosalind. "Allusion and Illusion in Donald Judd," *Artforum* 4 (May 1966)

Krauss, Rosalind. *Joel Shapiro*. Chicago: Museum of Contemporary Art, 1976

Krauss, Rosalind. *Passages in Modern Sculpture*. New York: Viking Press, 1977

Kubler, George. *The Shape of Time: Remarks on the History of Things*. New Haven, CT: Yale University Press, 1962

Legg, Alicia (ed.). *Sol LeWitt*. New York: Museum of Modern Art, 1978

LeWitt, Sol. *Geometric Figures and Color*. New York: Harry N. Abrams, 1979

Martin, Agnes, Richard Tuttle, and Michael Auping. *Agnes Martin/ Richard Tuttle*. Fort Worth, TX: Modern Art Museum of Fort Worth, 1998

Mayo, Marti. *Scott Burton: Chairs*. Cincinnati: The Contemporary Arts Center; Fort Worth, TX: The Fort Worth Art Museum, 1983

Merleau-Ponty, Maurice. *Phenomenology of Perception*. Translated by Colin Smith. London: Routledge & Kegan Paul, 1962

Meyer, James. *Minimalism: Art and Polemics in the Sixties*. New Haven, CT: Yale University Press, 2001

Meyer, Ursula. *Conceptual Art*. New York: Dutton, 1972

Naylor, Colin, and Genesis P-Orridge (eds.). *Contemporary Artists*. London: St. James Press, 1977

Noguchi, Isamu. *Isamu Noguchi: Space of Akari and Stone*. San Francisco: Chronicle Books, 1985

Noguchi, Isamu. *Isamu Noguchi: Sculptural Design*. Weil am Rhein: Vitra Design Museum, 2001

Ormond, Mark. *Joel Shapiro: Selected drawings, 1968–1990*. Miami, FL: Center for the Fine Arts, 1991

Perreault, John. *Usable Art*. Plattsburgh, NY: State University College, 1981

Phillips, Lisa. *Frederick Kiesler*. New York: Whitney Museum of American Art and W.W. Norton & Company, New York, 1989

Poling, Clark. *Kandinsky: Russian and Bauhaus Years, 1915–33*. New York: Solomon R. Guggenheim Museum, 1983

Possible Worlds: Sculpture from Europe. London: Institute of Contemporary Arts/Serpentine Gallery, 1990

Princenthal, Nancy. *Scott Burton: Chaise Longings*. New York: Max Protetch Gallery, 1996

Raskin, David Barry. "Donald Judd's Skepticism," Ph.D. diss., University of Texas at Austin, 1999

Richardson, Brenda, and Trish Waters. *Scott Burton*. Baltimore: Baltimore Museum of Art, 1986

Rose, Barbara. "ABC Art," *Art in America* 53, no. 5 (October/November 1965), pp. 57–69

Rothko, Mark, Yves Klein, and James Turrell. *On the Sublime: Mark Rothko, Yves Klein, James Turrell*. Berlin: Deutsche Guggenheim; New York: Solomon R. Guggenheim Museum, 2001

Rychlak, Bonnie. *Zen No Zen: Aspects of Noguchi's Sculptural Vision.* New York: Isamu Noguchi Foundation, 2002

Scott Burton: Sculpture Not Previously Exhibited. New York: Max Protetch Gallery, 1995

Shapiro, Joel. *Joel Shapiro: Sculpture in Clay, Plaster, Wood, Iron, and Bronze, 1971–1997.* Andover, MA: Addison Gallery of American Art, 1998

Shapiro, Joel, Richard Marshall, and Roberta Smith. *Joel Shapiro: Exhibition.* New York: Whitney Museum of American Art, 1982

Shapiro, Joel, and Pace Wildenstein Gallery. *Joel Shapiro: Recent Sculpture and Drawings.* New York: Pace Wildenstein Gallery, 2001

Shiff, Richard. "Donald Judd: Fast Thinking," *Donald Judd: Late Work.* New York: Pace Wildenstein Gallery, 2000

Silverman, Deborah. "Nature, Nobility, and Neurology: The Ideological Origins of 'Art Nouveau' in France," Ph.D. diss., Princeton University, 1983

Simon, Joan. "Sculpture as Theater," *Art in America* 91, no. 6 (June 2003), pp. 90–97, 137

Smith, Roberta. "Scott Burton: Designs on Minimalism," *Art in America* 66 (November/December 1978), pp. 138–40

Steinberg, Leo. *Encounters with Rauschenberg: A Lavishly Illustrated Lecture.* Houston, TX: The Menil Collection; Chicago and London: University of Chicago Press, 2000

Svestka, Jiri (ed.). *Scott Burton: Skupturen/Sculptures, 1980–89.* Düsseldorf: Kunstverein für die Rheinlande und Westfalen, 1989

Sylvester, Julie. *John Chamberlain: A Catalogue Raisonné of the Sculpture, 1954–1985.* Los Angeles: Museum of Contemporary Art and Hudson Hills Press, New York, 1986

Taragin, Davira S., Edward S. Cooke, Jr., and Joseph Giovannini. *Furniture by Wendell Castle.* Detroit: Founders Society, Detroit Institute of Arts and Hudson Hills Press, New York, 1989

Trockel, Rosemarie. *Rosemarie Trockel: Bodies of Work, 1986–1998; Köln, Brüssel, Paris, Wien I, Wien II, Opladen, Schwerte, Düren, Hamburg.* Cologne: Oktagon, 1998

Troy, Nancy. *Modernism and the Decorative Arts in France: Art Nouveau to Le Corbusier.* New Haven, CT: Yale University Press, 1991

Turrell, James. *James Turrell: Light and Space.* New York: Whitney Museum of American Art, 1980

Turrell, James. *James Turrell.* Paris: ARC, Musée d'Art Moderne de la Ville de Paris, 1983

Turrell, James, and Craig Adcock. *James Turrell: The Art of Light and Space.* Berkeley, CA: University of California Press, 1990

Turrell, James, Daniel Birnbaum, and Georges Didi-Huberman. *James Turrell: The Other Horizon.* Vienna: MAK, Österreichisches Museum für Angewandte Kunst, 1998

Tuttle, Richard. *Richard Tuttle: Wire Pieces.* Bordeaux: CAPC, Musée d'Art Contemporain, 1987

Tuttle, Richard. *Reading Red.* Cologne: König, 1998

Tuttle, Richard. *Replace the Abstract Picture Plane.* Photographic essay by Guido Baselgia. Edited by Matthias Haldemann. Zug: Kunsthaus Zug and Hatje Cantz Verlag, Ostfildern, 2001

Tuttle, Richard, and Marcia Tucker. *Richard Tuttle.* New York: Whitney Museum of American Art, 1975

Whiteread, Rachel. *Rachel Whiteread, Transient Spaces.* New York: Solomon R. Guggenheim Museum, 2001

Wilton-Ely, John. *Piranesi as Architect and Designer.* New Haven, CT: Yale University Press, 1993

INDEX

PHOTOGRAPHIC CREDITS

We are grateful to the following individuals and organizations for their permission to reproduce the images in this book. All images are referred to by figure number unless otherwise stated.

Addison Gallery of American Art, Phillips Academy: 26. Art Resource: 10, 147. Artes Magnus: 73, 119. Richard Artschwager/Artists Rights Society: 74–79. AXA Financial, Inc.: 182. BEYER: 62. Brooke Alexander Editions: 74, 79, 80, 138. Carnegie Museum of Art: 11. Carré d'Art-Musée d'art contemporain de Nîmes: 131. John Chamberlain/Artists Rights Society: 67–73. Chinati Foundation: 70, 117. Cleveland Museum of Art: 177. Christie's Images: 141, 146, 151, 155, 163, 167, 169, 171, 173, 175, 177. Cooper-Hewitt, National Design Museum, Smithsonian Institution: 3, 123. Elisabeth Cunnick/A/D Gallery: pp. 12–13; 12, 13, 14, 17, 22, 41, 54, 59, 60, 61, 63, 64, 68, 81, 85, 87, 120, 124, 129, 132, 168, 170, 172, 174, 176, 178, 183. David A. Hanks Associates: 179. Dia Art Foundation: 67, 114, 116, 133, 136. Dwan Gallery Archives: 71. Dwight Hackett Projects: 65. Equator Productions: 106. Estate of Scott Burton and Max Protetch Gallery: 45–53, 162, 164, 165, 167, 182. Dan Flavin/Artists Rights Society: 112–18. Fondazione Prada: 112. Friedrich Petzel Gallery: 135. Gagosian Gallery: 137. Gorney Bravin + Lee: 110, 111. Jaime Frankfurt: 156. Hirshhorn Museum and Sculpture Garden, Smithsonian Institution: 25. Bryan Hunt: 89–91. Indianapolis Museum of Art: 57. Irish Museum of Modern Art: 130. Isamu Noguchi Foundation, Inc.: 11, 12, 147. Istituto Nazionale per la Grafica, Rome: 4. Jewish Museum/Art Resource: 20, 21, 78. Judd Foundation/VAGA: 2, 8, 21–44, 139, 140, 149, 150, 152, 153, 154, 156, 159, 160, 181. Ellsworth Kelly: 15. Sol LeWitt/Artists Rights Society: 81–88. Magnum Photos: 6. Marion Goodman Gallery: 84. Matthew Marks Gallery: 16. Metropolitan Museum of Art: 158. Minneapolis Institute of Arts: 152, 179. Museum of the City of New York: 1. Museum of Contemporary Art, Los Angeles: 109. Museum of Modern Art/SCALA/Art Resource: 10, 148. Museum of South Texas, Corpus Christi: 35. Museum Villa Stuck, Munich, Germany: pp. 10–11; 180. nest magazine: 107, 125, 128. Nolan/Eckman Gallery: 104, 105. Claes Oldenburg: 19. Jorge Pardo: 134, 135. Paula Cooper Gallery: 77. Peabody Essex Museum: 5. Phillips, de Pury & Luxembourg: 7, 157, 161, 166. P.S. 1: 122. Richard Gray Gallery: 144. Tom Sachs: 126, 127. Joel Shapiro/Artists Rights Society: 92–98. Kiki Smith: 63. Solomon R. Guggenheim Museum: 118, 121. Sotheby's Inc.: 9, 32, 33. Sperone Westwater: 55, 56, 57, 58. Sprüth/Magers Gallery: 108. The Taunton Press, Inc.: 145. Treadway Gallery, Inc.: 171. Richard Tuttle: 66. VAGA: 10, 17, 18. Western Interiors and Design magazine: 30, 34, 40. Whitney Museum of American Art: 74. Robert Wilson: 100–102. PHOTOGRAPHERS: Richard Averill Smith: 1. © Andrew Garn: 22, 27, 29, 54, 60, 66, 99, 129, 172. © Lisa Eisner: 2, 36, 44, 181. © Barbara Bloemink: 159. © Hester + Hardaway: 30, 34, 40. © Ken Schles: 59, 63. © Bill Orcutt: 62. © Tad Wiley: 69. Katrin Schilling: pp. 10–11, 180. Robert McKeever: 137. Paola Bobba: 112. © Andrew Lawson: 103. © Michael Whiteway: 142. © Jerry Cohen: 143. Vytas Valaitis: 147. Mark Darley: 157.

The publishers have made every effort to trace and contact the copyright holders of the images reproduced in this book; they will be happy to correct in subsequent editions any errors or omissions that are brought to their attention.

First published 2004 by
Merrell Publishers Limited

Head office:
42 Southwark Street
London SE1 1UN

New York office:
49 West 24th Street
New York, NY 10010

www.merrellpublishers.com

in association with

Cooper-Hewitt, National Design Museum
Smithsonian Institution
2 East 91st Street
New York, NY 10128
www.cooperhewitt.org

Published on the occasion of the exhibition
Design ≠ Art: Functional Objects from Donald Judd to Rachel Whiteread organized by
Cooper-Hewitt, National Design Museum, Smithsonian Institution, New York
September 10, 2004 – February 27, 2005

Text copyright © 2004 Cooper-Hewitt, National Design Museum, Smithsonian Institution
"It's Hard to Find a Good Lamp" © Judd Foundation
Excerpt: "Situation Esthetics" © Estate of Scott Burton/Max Protetch Gallery, NY
Reprinted with permission of *Artforum*
"Thesis, Antithesis, Synthesis" © Richard Tuttle
Design and layout copyright © 2004 Merrell Publishers Limited

All rights reserved. No part of this publication may be reproduced,
stored in a retrieval system or transmitted, in any form or by any means,
electronic, mechanical, photocopying, recording or otherwise, without
the prior permission in writing from the publishers.

British Library Cataloging-in-Publication Data:
Bloemink, Barbara J.
Design – is not equal to – art : functional objects from Donald Judd to Rachel Whiteread
1.Design – History – 20th century 2.Minimal art
I.Title II.Cunningham, Joseph
745.4'09045

ISBN 1 85894 266 7 (hardcover edition)
ISBN 1 85894 267 5 (softcover edition)

A catalog record for this book is available from the Library of Congress.

Produced by Merrell Publishers Limited
Designed by mgmt. design: Alicia Yin Cheng and Sarah Gephart
Edited by Tom Neville and Simon Cowell
Printed and bound in Hong Kong

Jacket front: Donald Judd, *Frame Corner Chair #72*, 1990. Oak
Jacket back: Rachel Whiteread, installation view, *Daybed*, A/D Gallery, New York, 2000.
Beech wood and multi-density foams with wool upholstery